Sales Taxation

The Case of Value Added Tax in the European Community

Series on International Taxation

This book, *Sales Taxation*, is the eighth in the 'Series on International Taxation' published by Kluwer Law and Taxation Publishers.

This series of books is intended for use by those engaged in the practice of international taxation. The books are of high quality.

Other titles in this series:

1. Professor Alberto Xavier, *The Taxation of Foreign Investment in Brazil*
2. Professor Hugh J. Ault/Dr Albert J. Rädler, *The German Corporation Tax Law with 1980 Amendments*
3. Professor Paul R. McDaniel/Hugh J. Ault, *Introduction to United States International Taxation*
4. Professor Dr Albert J. Rädler, *German Transfer Pricing/Prix de Transfer en Allemagne*
5. Professor Paul R. McDaniel/Stanley S. Surrey, *International Aspects of Tax Expenditures: A Comparative Study*
6. Dr C. van Raad, *Nondiscrimination in International Tax Law*
7. Professor Sijbren Cnossen (ed.), *Tax Coordination in the European Community*

Sales Taxation

The Case of Value Added Tax in the European Community

BEN TERRA

Professor in Law
Universities of Amsterdam and Leyden

SERIES ON INTERNATIONAL TAXATION, NO. 8

Kluwer Law and Taxation Publishers
Deventer · Boston

Distribution in the USA and Canada
Kluwer Law and Taxation Publishers
101 Philip Drive
Norwell, MA 02061

Library of Congress Cataloging in Publication Data

Terra, B. J. M.
  Sales Taxation: the case of value added tax in the European community / Ben Terra.
  p. cm. — (Series on international taxation; no. 8)
  Includes index.
  ISBN 9065443819
  1. Value-added tax—Law and legislation—European Economic Community countries.
  2. Sales tax—Law and legislation—European Economic Community countries.
I. Title. II. Series.
KJE7285.T47 1988
343.405′5—dc 19
[344.0355]   88-13584
                                                                              CIP

D 1988/2664/74

ISBN 90 6544 381 9

© 1988 Kluwer Law and Taxation Publishers

Preface

This book is divided into two parts: the first part is devoted to the theory of sales taxes, Value Added Tax (VAT) in particular, as general indirect taxes on consumption. The second part deals with the VAT in the European Community, focusing on the efforts to remove the fiscal barriers caused by the present VAT in Europe. Finally it briefly touches upon the differences between retail sales taxes, as applied for example in the USA, and the European VAT. It is argued that in the final analysis VAT is the superior method of taxation. This book is to a large extent a reproduction of my lectures on VAT presented, as a visiting professor, at the University of Florida in Gainesville during the 1987 Fall semester.

This book is meant to be a textbook for students who are interested in more than their national sales taxation alone. It is also written for those (tax-lawyers, accountants and other practitioners) who deal with sales taxes in their day-to-day practice and who want to obtain a better understanding of the similarities between various sales tax legislations.

In composing this book a choice had to be made from an overwhelming variety of subjects and materials. It will be clear that the choice made by the writer represents his personal preference reflecting his interest and priorities.

Ben Terra
Gainesville
July 1988

Acknowledgements

During the Fall Semester 1987, I lectured in Gainesville, Florida in an exchange program between the University of Florida and the University of Leyden. The various chapters of this book were written in preparation for the lectures (26 in total).

I am greatly indebted to Prof. J. Reugebrink, whose leading textbook on Value Added Tax (*Omzetbelasting*, Deventer 1985) has been my guide in the theoretical aspects of sales taxation, (as this has been the case during my studies at the University of Leyden). I am grateful for his permission to publish specifically the Chapters IV and VI that are heavily drawn on Chapters 3 and 6 in his textbook. Chapter XI is originally a co-production with J.B. v.d. Zanden, director of the department of commodity taxes at the Ministry of Finance in the Hague. I appreciate his permission to publish this chapter.

I feel greatly indebted to all authors, whose articles and books I had a chance to consult and refer to, especially (in Chapter XIII) the recent publications by Prof. S. Cnossen.

I sincerely thank the students for their questions and remarks. Finally this book would never have been written without the patient typing and retyping by the secretary of the tax department at the University of Florida, Lena Hinson.

The aforementioned persons have contributed to enlarging this book's strengths. I take sole reponsibility for its weaknesses.

Ben Terra
Professor of Law
Universities of Amsterdam and Leyden

Table of Contents

PART TWO. COORDINATION OF VALUE ADDED TAXES
IN THE EUROPEAN COMMUNITY

Part One

Theoretical Aspects

of

Sales Taxation

and

Value Added Tax

Chapter I. Introduction

I.1 GENERAL

Although the concept of a sales tax is readily apparent, its coverage, the systems of levying and even the name may vary.[1] Through the ages governments have covered their spending partially by sales taxes, under various names. The roots of these taxes can be found in ancient civilizations.[2] The Romans applied a general sales tax to goods sold in markets or by auction.[3] They carried that system to Egypt, France, and Spain, and sales taxation continued in those territories after the fall of the Roman Empire. Sales taxes were widely used in Europe during the Middle Ages and later, especially in Spain where the *alcabala* was applied on a national scale as far back as the fourteenth century and was afterwards introduced in various countries under Spanish influence.[4] The Spanish efforts to introduce in the Netherlands a 10 per cent sales tax (the 'tenth penny') led to the Dutch revolt and consequently the independency of the Dutch provinces.[5] In fact, sales taxes carry with them a 'fate' that in almost all countries introduction of these taxes is related to trouble and sorrow.[6] It is not exaggerating to consider these taxes as the Germans call them *'Kinder der Not'* (children of despair) or as *'Krisen-, Kriegs- und Nachkriegssteuern'* (crisis, war, and after-war taxes).[7]

---

1. In addition to sales tax, 'turnover tax' or even 'general excise' is used. We will confine ourselves to the name sales tax. A sales tax may be defined by its legal character: a general indirect tax on consumption, *see infra* Chapter II.
2. *See generally*: R. Grabower, *Die Umsatzsteuer. Ihre Geschichte und Gegenwartigen Gestaltung im In- und Ausland*, Köln 1962 and J.C.L. Huiskamp, *De Omzetbelasting in internationaal verband*, Deventer 1966.
3. *See* J.C.L. Huiskamp, *De Omzetbelasting in internationaal verband*, Deventer 1966.
4. *See* 'Sales Tax Administration: Major structural and practical issues with special reference to the needs of developing countries'. United Nations, Department of Economic and Social Affairs, New York 1976, p.4. (Hereafter: Sales Tax Administration/UN-study).
5. This 'monstrous levy' played an important role in arousing support for the revolt. *See* G. Parker, *The Dutch Revolt*, London 1979, pp 114–115. *See generally* F.H.M. Grapperhaus, *Alva en de tiende penning*, Zutphen 1982.
6. *See* J. Reugebrink, *Omzetbelasting*, Deventer 1985, p. 1.
7. *See* Grabower, *op. cit.* note 2 *supra*, in its foreword by Popitz.

3

Especially the modern[8] sales taxes are related with war and crises. This can be seen from the dates on which the taxes were introduced : Germany in 1916 in the middle of the First World War in order to cover the ever increasing government spending resulting from this war; in France in 1920 and in Belgium in 1921, in both cases to cover the disastrous effects of this war. In England the purchase tax, a system of general excises, was introduced in 1940 (a system that as a whole can be considered as a sales tax). The problem in England was 'How to pay for the war'. In the Netherlands, a manufacturers sales tax was introduced in 1933; in the same year a general retail sales tax became effective in Pennsylvania. During the next six years, twenty-six American states (and Hawaii) imposed a general sales tax.[9] The reasons for the introduction of these taxes fell into a major pattern. The depression reduced revenues from other taxes at the same time that relief needs were increasing.[10] The sales tax, with its low rate, large yield and relatively painless collection, was especially attractive.

Also the post-war period shows a trend toward adoption of sales taxes in virtually all countries in the world.[11] In fact, sales taxes have become indispensable for governments to cover their expenses.[12]

---

8. The present sales taxes are modern and not a heritage of the past, since in the eighteenth and nineteenth centuries with the rise of the doctrine of taxation according to the ability to pay, sales taxes gradually gave way to primitive forms of taxes on earnings and property combined with specific duties for customs and excises, so that by the beginning of the twentieth century they played only a minor role in the tax system of the few countries that still retained them. *See* Sales Tax Administration/UN-study, p. 4.

9. Although six were allowed to expire after one or two years (Pennsylvania, Idaho, Kentucky, Maryland, New Jersey and New York) *see* John F. Due and John L. Mikesell, *Sales Taxation. State and Local Structure and Administration*, Baltimore, London 1983, p. 2.

10. For the American States it may be added concurrently, the serious financial difficulties of the local governments, greatly aggravated by the depression, resulted in a tendency both to increase state grants to the local governments, particularly for education, and to reduce reliance on the property tax. Most states had few major sources that could yield additional revenues. Their income taxes, particularly, reflected the decline in personal incomes. Due/Mikesell, *idem.*

11. As of 1 July 1987, a general sales tax was in operation in 45 states of the US. *See generally* S. Cnossen, *Excise systems; A global study of the selective taxation of goods and services.* Baltimore 1977. Countries which have recently introduced a VAT include Argentina, Bolivia, Brazil, Chile, Columbia, Costa Rica, Dominican Republic, Ecuador, Guatemala, Haiti, Honduras, Indonesia, Israel, Ivory Coast, Korea, Madagascar, Mexico, Morocco, New Zealand, Niger, Nicaragua, Panama, Peru, Senegal and Uruguay. The People's Republic of China adopted VAT in a restricted form in 1984, this being the first example of its application in a socialist country. *See* Li Jinyan, 'People's Republic of China, Value Added Tax', *Bulletin for International Fiscal Documentation*, January 1988.

12. The rise of (general) sales taxes in developing countries is also triggered by the lowering yields of customs duties, caused by the gradual reductions of the rates as a result of the multilateral trade negotiations conducted under the auspices of the GATT. Also, as the economy of a country develops, customs duties represent a progressively less productive and less acceptable source of revenue. *See* Sales Tax Administration/UN-study, p. 3.

I.2 LEGAL CHARACTER

The purpose of a sales tax is, in short, to tax goods destined for personal consumption; in other words it taxes goods on their way to a consumer. Also, services can and in my opinion should be included. This does not mean that all taxes that tax goods and services on their way to a consumer possess the same legal character. The legal character of a tax may be defined as features (or the nature) of a tax that (ought to) have consequences *in iure*.[13] The reason why the goods are taxed in various tax systems can be very different. For example, sales taxes can be distinguished from business occupation taxes. Business occupation taxes are regarded as levies on the business, *per se*. In other words the business activities are at the center rather than the (kind of) goods or services, as in a sales tax. It is important to determine the legal character of a tax. The legislative structure and the interpretation of terminology shoul be guided by the legal character.

For example, one of the consequences of a tax being a business occupation tax is that this tax is not expected to be passed forward to the purchaser. At least this is not the original understanding. So when the tax cannot be passed forward e.g. because of a tax-raise combined with a price freeze, there is no legal basis for complaint. The case is different, if this happened in a sales tax. In fact, it ceases to be wholly a general tax on consumption and becomes, at least in part, the equivalent of a direct tax on business enterprises.[14] The legal character of a sales tax can be described as a 'general indirect tax on consumption'. This is not only a name, but also provides the legal character of the tax.[15] The consequences of this character are manifold. They will be discussed in the following chapter.

I.3 TAX ON CONSUMPTION

A tax on consumption aims at taxing the expenditure by private persons. 'Private persons' should not be taken literally. In most taxes on consumption the expenditures by churches, by the government, in short by all non-entrepreneurs are also taxed.[16]

Ideas about the concept of a tax on consumption have changed in recent times. Not too long ago it was thought that a tax on consumption should cover not only consumption in a more literal sense, like ingestion and in general the 'using-up' of products, but also the mere usage – or application – of goods.

13. Not that these consequences are necessarily enforceable.
14. *See* Sales Tax Administration/UN-study, p. 2.
15. *See* J. Reugebrink, 'The Sixth Directive for Harmonization of Value Added Tax', C.M.L.Rev. 1978, p. 309.
16. J. Reugebrink, *op. cit.* note 5 *supra*, p. 3.

The character of the tax should therefore result in taxation not only of the consumption of goods by private persons, but also in taxation of the use of machines, means of transportation and other means of production. This idea can be found in the so-called income type of value added tax (*see further* Chapter V.3.2). These ideas have largely disappeared and the general opinion about a tax on consumption is that the tax is meant to cover the expenditures by private persons and persons comparable to them.[17] Nonetheless, producer goods still are taxed under sales taxes, mainly because taxing them provides for a lower rate of tax than exempting them.[18]

One could say it is only for technical reasons that the tax is not levied directly from private consumers. In my view this ideal, direct taxation upon the private consumer, should be borne in mind when designing an efficient indirect tax on consumption.[19] We will return to this starting point when we consider the legal character in the following chapter.

---

17. C.P. Tuk, *Wet op de omzetbelasting 1968*, Deventer 1970, p. 29.
18. *See* Sales Tax Administration/UN-report, p. 35.
19. Therefore, in my view it is (for example) acceptable to designate, on an occasional basis, private consumers as taxable persons contrary to the *indirect* character of a tax on consumption if this provision makes the taxation more efficient.

Chapter II. General Indirect Tax on Consumption

II.1 INTRODUCTION

Sales taxes can be levied in various ways, for example, in a direct way, or in an indirect way as a retail sales tax or as a value added tax. (In Chapters IV and V a survey of the indirect systems will be offered.) It, however, is not the technique of levying a tax, but its legal character which decides whether a tax is a sales tax. This legal character, previously defined as the features (or the nature) of a tax that (ought to) have consequences *in iure*, may at first seem a somewhat esoteric concept. Basically it means that the intrinsic nature of a tax should be the guiding principle in determining its consequences and not just the label, or the name of a tax. Still the design of a tax by a legislator may have, from the point of legislative intent, certain consequences and usually will do so, even when certain rules are against the very concept of the tax as referred to originally by the legislator. Clearly when a legislator excludes certain transactions from a tax that has been announced as a *general tax* on consumption, this is 'intentional' and not – so to speak – 'illegal'. However, when a legislator explicitly (or implicitly) expresses his intention to introduce a certain tax, perhaps by labelling it as such, but the nature of the tax enacted is clearly different from its label, the legal character of the tax itself can very well be decisive of certain consequences. For example the consequences (regarding border tax adjustments) are different for a tax having the nature of a business occupation tax than for a tax that can be characterized as an indirect sales tax, whatever name is given to the tax. In the former case the adjustments are forbidden by international regulations, in the latter they are permissable. (*See further* Chapter IX *infra.*) The concept of the legal character as a guiding principle is not only a matter of *a posteriori* concern; once a tax has been introduced, unresolved questions should be answered by searching the very nature of the tax, again unless political decisions – for example notable from the preparatory works – compel[1] deviations from the character of the tax. The legal character also ought to be a matter of *a fortiori* concern; when designing a tax it should be the guiding principle, without becoming an

---

1. That is as long as the judiciary is willing to uphold the original understanding.

unbearable 'bodice'. The nature of a tax should offer an optimal model, from which deviations should be permitted only after full debate in order to avoid a tax law representing a patchwork of (often short-term) political interests.

I believe that universally the legal character of a sales tax can be described as a *general indirect tax on consumption.*[2] The consequences of this character are manifold. To each of the elements we will now pay separate attention.

II.2 GENERAL TAX

A sales tax is a general tax on consumption; general as distinct from specific. Excises are examples of specific taxes.

A sales tax is intended to tax *all* private expenditure. One result of this view is that a sales tax should not discriminate between goods and services, as they both represent consumption. This makes good sense, since in many instances a certain good is a close substitute for a particular service. For example, one can replace some parts on a car or have them rebuilt. One can buy a washing machine or have one's laundry done by a third party. Taxing the purchase of goods – the parts or the washing machine – and not taxing the close substitute services – the rebuilding or laundry service – discriminates against the purchase of goods and abandons a good portion of the tax base for no good reason.[3] Nevertheless, many legislators hesitate to include services. This hesitancy in taxing services may be attributed to three factors.[4]

First the difficulty of selecting the services to be taxed. To tax services that are used to an appreciable degree by businesses would sometimes – depending on the system of levying (*see* Chapter IV and V *infra*) – result in double taxation, while taxing non-business services of an educational, medical or social nature has always been felt undesirable.

Second, it has been the general notion that to tax services would be tantamount to taxing labor, which was believed to be inappropriate in a tax intended primarily to apply to consumer goods.

Third, there is the problem that, because services are provided by small one-man enterprises, some of which might escape 'detection', a tax on services might be discriminatory. In my view these arguments against inclusion of services in a sales tax do not counterbalance the substitution problem caused by only taxing (the delivery of) goods.

A further justification for taxing services, one of particular relevance in developing countries, is that because expenditure on services generally forms a larger proportion to the total expenditure of higher income groups than of

---

2. *See* for this conclusion regarding the European sales taxation (VAT and its predecessors, which widely differed from each other) Chapter VIII *infra*.
3. *Cf.* G. Mundstock, 'Florida Services: You only tax twice?' *Tax Notes* 1987, p. 1137.
4. Sales Tax Administration/UN-study, p. 72.

lower-income groups, taxing services makes a sales tax less regressive in its incidence.[5]

From the general aspect of the legal character also the next legitimate requirement follows. Since a general tax on consumption is a tax on the expenditure of individual consumers, as a matter of course there should be a relation between the tax burden and the quantity of the expenditure. A minimal requirement, legitimate in taxation, is that the amount of tax payable is *measurable* as per individual taxpayer.[6] In order to connect the expenditure of individual consumers with the tax burden, it is necessary that the amount of tax payable is certain, as a percentage of the retail price. The amount has to be *equal* for identical goods. In other words a sales tax has to be measurable, so the tax burden can be distributed as intended. This can only (fully) be realized if the tax consists of a previously determined percentage of the (retail) price. As will be seen in Chapter IV, this cannot be guaranteed in cumulative cascade systems.

Thus the general character of a sales tax demands that the equal is treated equally and the unequal in proportion unequally. This theory of tax justice is the general principle guiding the distribution of a nation's tax liabilities among individual taxpayers. If generally accepted, it is one of the most important standards for judging a tax measure or a system of taxes. Almost all tax authorities have emphasized this criterion of justice.[7] Moreover, 'equality' comes first on the list of maxims enumerated by Adam Smith in his *Inquiry into the Nature and Causes of the Wealth of Nations*.[8]

From the equality requirement it follows that it should not make any difference whether an expenditure is related to goods produced in the country of consumption or to imported goods. A tentative conclusion therefore is that a sales tax comprises a (compensatory) tax on importation, since otherwise private consumers do not pay (any) tax, whenever foreign products are concerned.[9] This conclusion is based on the starting point that imported products have left the foreign country 'tax-free'. This starting-point is closely connected with the indirect character of the sales tax. (*See further* Section II.4.)

---

5. *Idem.*
6. J. Reugebrink, *Enkele beschouwingen over de neutraliteit van de omzetbelasting*. Openbare les. Deventer 1965. p. 7.
7. Clara K. Sullivan, *The Tax on Value Added*, New York 1965, p. 151.
8. *An inquiry into the Nature and Causes of the Wealth of Nations*, the Modern Library, New York 1937. p. 777.
9. This argument is based on the 'consumer-cost-profit-doctrine', R.W. Rosendahl, 'Border tax adjustments: problems and proposals'. *Law and Policy in International Business* 1970, p. 91: 'Since the consumer bears the burden of these indirect taxes, they should at the same time be the beneficiaries of the government services which these taxes finance. Hence the tax revenues should accrue to the government which these taxes finance'. *See also* the benefit-principle under Chapter X.3 *infra*.

II.3 CONSUMPTION

A sales tax is a tax on consumption. As an indication of the character of the tax the word consumption may cause misunderstandings. Some goods can be consumed fully and immediately like a glass of milk or a sandwich. The consumption of other goods is a continuous process. These goods are used up only in the long run or hardly ever at all like a piece of art, or immovable property. A sales tax should not be concerned with 'consumption' in this (two-fold) sense. Instead, the expenditure, in order to attain consumption, is the relevant consideration. A distinction between immediate and continuous use or consumption is not to be made. The tax is due as soon as the consumer has made the expenditure, the tax is levied from the person with whom the money has been spent. Basically the tax is not concerned with the 'adventures' of the product; whether the milk is consumed or has turned sour or whether the immovable property burns down has no effect. Only in specific circumstances, for example, when the product does not meet the promised standards and is (in an unused condition) returned immediately the transaction will be considered not to have taken place and will be 'reversed'.

The conclusion can be drawn that in a general tax on consumption the following consistent rule applies: 'consumption is expenditure', in other words 'all consumption is an immediate event'.[10] To this conclusion it should be added that a general tax on consumption distinguishes between consumptive and productive expenditure.[11] Such a tax only intends to tax private consumption. Even this restriction does not solve all problems, especially when products are not 'fully used'. When these products are transferred from one consumer to another, theoretically, no problems arise.[12] The goods remain in the sphere of consumers.[13] When a private consumer transfers the goods to another private consumer, the goods stay in the consumers' sphere. Generally the tax is only levied at entrepreneurs and the like. If used products are sold to a dealer, they return to the business sphere. In his price to the dealer, the consumer will take into account part of the tax that he considers 'not to be consumed'. Upon sale by the dealer to another consumer, again tax

---

10. A.F. Ploeger, 'Het verbruik in de omzetbelasting', W.F.R. 1972, p. 969.
11. J. Reugebrink, *Omzetbelasting*, Deventer 1985, p. 7.
12. In at least one Member State of the European Community (Germany) serious effects are caused by the competition-distortion, since a sale by a private household is not taxable. *See* D. Pohmer, Germany, p. 172 in H.J. Aaron (ed), *The Value Added Tax: Lessons from Europe*, Washington 1981.
13. The delimitation of consumption has been referred to as one of the weaknesses in value added taxation (Pohmer, *op. cit.* previous note, p. 171). Since the tax generally is not levied directly from private consumers (except on occasion of importation of goods), it does not mean that the tax can *never* be levied from private consumers. Bearing in mind that the ideal starting-point is a direct taxation of the private consumer, I believe it is occasionally acceptable.

is due. Thus, in a certain way cumulation of tax occurs. The problem is that regarding the same product tax is levied again. From a theoretical point of view this presents no difficulties. When consumption is an immediate event, the conclusion is that this immediate event may occur more than once.

In sales tax systems this paradigm is not always upheld. The consequences of consumption are *mitigated* on several occasions, especially in case of exchange of secondhand products.[14] For example, in order to avoid tendencies to exclude dealers in trading secondhand goods, dealers may be allowed to deduct from the tax base the value of the traded in secondhand good. It is also possible to include private consumers in the levy of the tax regarding the sale of certain secondhand goods.

Besides measures taken to mitigate the consequences of consumption, an outright *exception* is made in the case of import or export by private consumers.[15] In these cases theory[16] conflicts with the principle of the country of destination, a principle which is closely linked to the indirect character of a sales tax, the subject to which we turn now.

II.4 INDIRECT

Theoretically it is conceivable that a tax on consumption is levied directly from the consumer. Such a tax has been defended by Nicholas Kaldor in his book *An Expenditure Tax*.[17] Such a direct tax has nowhere proven its efficiency. Universally, taxes on consumption are levied indirectly.

14. Other possible mitigations are the previously mentioned reversion of the transaction in the case of returning unused goods and the treatment of deliveries and leasing or letting of immovable property, *see infra* Chapter VIII.
15. This exception amounts to the non-taxation in the country of expenditure from where the goods are exported. The expenditure is taxed upon importation in the country of destination. In some cases a 'travelers exemption' is applied, thus no tax on importation is levied – notwithstanding the 'general' character of the tax – since the expenditure (the consumption) is deemed to have taken place in the country from which the goods are exported. This ambivalent approach is clearly inconsistent with the destination principle discussed under II.4 *infra. See further* Chapter IX.
16. The question arises whether the rule 'consumption is expenditure' is valid, since it is mitigated and even an outright exception is made in the case of import and export by private consumers. In my opinion it is. Doctrines like taxation according to the ability to pay do not fit into a sales tax. Sales taxation should not be viewed separated from, but in combination with other forms of taxation, especially income taxation. Sales taxation deals with the *expenditure*-side, of course, in relation to the income-side, the *private* expenditure-side. The results of these expenditures are, in principle, not relevant, even if consumption is renounced, or impossible. The fact that in certain cases a theoretical starting-point is not applied does not falsify the assumption, it (re)affirms the fact that principles are relative. Not all that is justified in theory should therefore be applied. The function of principles is to guide, not to be(come) a 'bodice'. In what follows it will be assumed that 'consumption is expenditure'.
17. London, 1955.

The Oxford English Dictionary defines an indirect tax as one which is 'not levied directly upon the person on whom it ultimately falls, but charged in some other way, especially upon the production or importation of articles of use or consumption, the price of which is thereby augmented to the consumer, who thus pays the tax in the form of increased price'.

The definition of indirect taxes, and their differences from direct taxes, is based on the assumption regarding the shifting of the tax, that is, that indirect taxes are fully shifted forward to the consumer and thus are fully reflected in the sales price, and that direct taxes are fully shifted backward to the producer and thus have no price effect whatsoever.[18]

Economists have challenged the validity of these assumptions. As early as 1964 a meeting of economists in Paris reached the consensus that 'In practice indirect taxes are not fully shifted forward in product prices possibly because of the fall in factor prices, tax evasion, or other causes.'[19] The view also merged that direct taxes like the corporation profits tax may be partially shifted into product prices, and that this tendency is more likely perhaps in the United States than in Europe.[20]

Since assumptions of complete forward and backward shifting are an inadequate approximation of reality, it has been suggested that the classification of taxes as indirect or direct has hardly any scientific value.[21] Nevertheless, the distinction is important in two respects.

In the first place, a legal consequence is connected to the qualification of a tax as indirect. Even if from an economic point of view, an indirect tax cannot be fully shifted forward and direct taxes are not fully shifted backward – contrary to the intentions of the legislator so to speak – still the legal character of 'indirect taxes' requires the *possibility* of shifting forward the indirect tax. Thus the legislator has to see to it that shifting is possible. In any case the shifting should not be hindered. In other words, from the indirect character of a tax the necessity follows that the tax may not influence competition. The amount of tax may not be influenced by the extent of vertical or horizontal integration, since the resulting different tax burdens may ensure that the business firm that has to pay the highest tax cannot fully shift the tax burden forward.[22]

The second reason that prevents the classification between direct and

---

18. *Cf.* Rosendahl, *op. cit.* note 9 *supra*, p. 90.
19. M. Leontiades, 'The Logic of Border Taxes', *National Tax Journal*, 1966, p. 173.
20. *Idem.* Due, however, states referring to the VAT: 'Under reasonable assumptions, it is likely that the tax does tend to be reflected in consumer prices, and the separate quotation probably facilitates exact shifting. But it is hard to believe that there are no exceptions . . .' J.F. Due, 'The Universality and Neutrality of the Value Added Tax reexamined'. Taxes – *The Tax Magazine* 1977, p. 472.
21. H.J. Hofstra, *Inleiding tot het Nederlands belastingrecht*, Deventer 1977, p. 39.
22. *See* the effect of cumulative cascade systems under Chapter IV *infra*.

indirect taxation from being rendered out of date is the so-called destination principle.[23] As a tentative conclusion of the general character of a tax on consumption, it was suggested that it should not make any difference, whether the expenditure is related to goods produced in the country of consumption or to imported goods (*see* Section II.2 *supra*). It was concluded that, therefore, a sales tax comprises a (compensatory) tax on importation, since otherwise private consumers do not pay (any) tax, whenever foreign products are consumed. This conclusion is not inevitable. It is possible that imported products are already taxed in the country of production, so that a compensatory tax on importation leads to double taxation. In that case the general character of a tax on consumption would, to the contrary, resist such a compensatory levy! The question of double taxation depends on the degree of tax coordination between states. It depends on the accepted system of allocation of the taxes. An important aspect in this field is also the degree of political and economic cooperation between states; whether this cooperation has features of a federal or confederal state or of an economic community. Additionally the system of levying a sales tax (multiple or single-retail stage) influences the double taxation effects. We will return to this subject later. In practice, double sales taxation between independent states is to a large extent avoided, since for indirect taxes the country of destination has been accepted as the leading principle.

This so-called 'destination principle' taxes goods where they are 'consumed', refunding the tax on export goods and imposing tax on imports. Alternatively, the 'origin principle' taxes goods where they are produced. Thus exports are taxed, and imports are exempt under this principle.

The disadvantage of the origin principle is that the tax burden on imported products and on locally produced products is not necessarily the same, notably when in the country of origin a different rate is applied. Imported products from a low-tax country may distort competition, causing trade deficits.[24] As a result the country of importation, the high-tax country, will have to take steps to counteract this effect.[25] Therefore the principle of origin is only suitable for application between countries with identical, or closely similar, tax systems and sales tax rates.[26]

Application of the destination principle leads to compensation in the form of a surcharge on imports, not exceeding the internal tax on corresponding domestic products. The imported products cross the border 'tax-free' since on

23. J. Reugebrink, 'Directe en indirecte belastingen een achterhaalde classificatie?', p. 135 in: A.K.P. Jongsma and J. Verburg (ed.), *Cijns en Dijns*, Deventer 1975.
24. Small differences in rates may be absorbed by higher transportation costs. A.J. Easson, *Tax law and policy in the EEC*, London 1980, p. 60.
25. This counteraction may be a reduction of the real costs of domestic production on the rate of exchange of its currency. Easson, *op. cit.* previous note, p. 60.
26. *Idem.*

exportation the tax already borne by the article in the country of production has been refunded.[27]

The advantage of the destination principle is that all products bear the same tax burden when finally sold to the consumer. The disadvantage is that border tax adjustments always seem necessary.

The destination principle applies to indirect taxes.[28] Herein lies the main importance of the classification of taxes as indirect taxes. Since the economic significance of the distribution between direct and indirect taxes is doubtful, caused by imperfect shifting, the determination of a tax as indirect is the sole decisive factor whether the destination principle may be applied.

The destination principle is recognized in the General Agreement on Tariffs and Trade. We will return to the GATT under Part Two, Chapter IX.

---

27. Reality is more complicated. Goods may carry a tax burden, e.g. caused by exemptions granted in previous stages of production or distribution. *See* Chapter VI *infra*.
28. Rosendahl, *op. cit.* note 9 *supra*, p. 98: 'The GATT-rules have incorporated the country of destination principle of tax treatment for the indirect taxes.'

Chapter III. Neutrality

The observation has been made that:

'The importance of border adjustments . . . depends on their effect on international trade. If the exclusion of indirect taxes on exports adjusts prices solely by the amount of the tax, and imports bear the same tax as similar domestically produced goods the border tax mechanism would be neutral'.[1]

The question which arises is: neutral as regards what?

Neutrality of taxation is a relative matter.[2] Relativity is to be understood in its literal sense: neutrality can only be considered in relation to certain indicated phenomena.

Neutral effects in international trade may be with regard to competition, the balance of payment or, in general, economic relations.

However, neutrality may also be characterized by legal relationship, for example, through equality of tax payers.

In order to discuss neutrality in a relative perspective it is useful to discern two different levels of neutrality: internal and external neutrality. Internal neutrality can be divided into legal, economic and competition neutrality.[3]

III.1 INTERNAL NEUTRALITY

One aspect of the internal neutrality is legal neutrality. The *legal neutrality* of a sales tax is connected to the legal character of this tax. This legal character has been dealt with separately (under Chapter II). It was concluded that, since a general tax on consumption is a tax on the expenditure of individual

---

1. M. Leontiades, 'The logic of border taxes', *National Tax Journal* 1966, p. 173.
2. *Cf.* C.P. Tuk, *Wet op de omzetbelasting 1968*, Deventer 1979, p. 45.
   As a matter of fact 'There is no such thing as a truly "neutral" tax system': A. Easson, 'Fiscal discrimination: New perspectives on article 95 of the EEC Treaty', C. M. L. Rev. 1981, p. 521.
3. J. Reugebrink, *Enkele beschouwingen over de neutraliteit van de omzetbelasting*. Openbare les. Deventer 1965. *See also* M.E. Möller, 'On the Value Added Tax in Denmark and the Economic Community and the Renaissance of Tax Neutrality', *Bulletin of International Fiscal Documentation*, October 1967, pp. 431–450.

consumers, as a matter of course there should be a relation between the tax burden and the quantity of the expenditure.[4] A minimal requirement, legitimate in taxation, is that the amount of tax payable is measurable as per individual taxpayer.

In order to connect the expenditure of individual consumers with the tax burden, it is necessary that the amount of tax payable is certain, as a percentage of the retail price; the amount has to be equal for identical products.[5] In order to be considered legally neutral, a sales tax has to be measurable, so the tax burden can be distributed as intended. This can only be realised if the tax consists of a previously determined percentage of the (retail) price.

In cumulative cascade tax systems legal neutrality can never be guaranteed.[6] In such systems tax is imposed on all or at several stages of the production and distribution chain. At each stage the tax is cumulated.[7] Vertical and horizontal integration of production and distribution results in a reduction of taxes under the cumulative cascade system. The tax burden on a given product cannot be determined exactly because a product may have different producers with varying levels of integration and therefore carries different tax burdens.

Cumulative cascade systems do not offer legal neutrality.

The *competition neutrality* is also based on a relation with the retail price.[8]

When the tax burden does not depend on the extent of vertical or horizontal integration, but is formed by a previously fixed percentage of the retail price, concentration in businesses will not be (tax) advantageous. Thus, if a sales tax is legally neutral, competition will not be distorted; the tax will be 'competition neutral'.

Competition neutrality is not just a matter of economics. A legal aspect is formed by the intention of the legislator.[9] An indirect general tax on consumption is meant to be paid by business firms, but the tax must be borne by individuals, the consumers. The business firms merely serve as convenient

---

4. This 'matter of course' is based on the principle of equity which is indispensable as basic norm to protect taxation from '*Willkür und Zufall*' (arbitrariness and coincidence). *Cf.* H.J. Hofstra, 'Over belastingbeginselen', WFR 1979, p. 1219.
5. Reugebrink, *op. cit.* note 3 *supra*, p. 7.
6. *See* Chapter IV, *infra*.
7. Or 'pyramided' *see* R.W. Rosendahl, 'Border tax adjustments: problems and proposals', *Law and Policy in International Business* 1970, p. 101.
8. Reugebrink, *op. cit.* note 3 *supra*, p. 7.
9. The impact point of a tax burden is called the place of statutory incidence. The final resting point is the place of economic incidence. It is the distribution of the burden (after shifting) that counts. 'If this distribution is to be as intended, legislators must choose tax formulas which give the desired result in terms not of statutory incidence but of the economic incidence' R.A. Musgrave and P.B. Musgrave, *Public finance in theory and practice*, New York 1976, p. 377.

collection points and are meant to pass the tax forward to the consumer in the form of higher prices.[10] This process is generally referred to as 'shifting'.

When a different tax burden, caused by a varying extent of integration, is borne by identical products, the business firm that has to pay the highest tax cannot fully shift the tax burden forward, if the firm wants to remain competitive. The firm will have to bear part of the tax burden itself. This is contrary to the legal intentions of the legislator.

ξ. The third form of internal neutrality is *economic neutrality*.[11] Here, a sales tax is considered neutral if the tax does not interfere with the optimal allocation of the means of production.[12] Such an interference may be caused by different rates in sales tax. Normally, the market mechanism allocates the provision of products and means of production.[13] Different tax rates influence this mechanism, that is, in so far as the demand is (completely) elastic to price.

In order to obtain an optimal economic neutrality the next principle should be borne in mind: apart from measures purposely taken by the legislator for political or other reasons, levying of taxes should not damage economic interests, therefore interference with the existing market mechanism should be kept to a minimum.[14]

The interference with the existing market (or price) mechanism caused by different sales tax rates does not necessarily lead to the conclusion of one uniform rate, since the legislator is entitled to interfere with the price mechanism for political or other reasons. An important reason for such an action is considered to be the regressivity of the sales tax. 'A sales tax is regressive since the ratio of consumption to income (the average propensity to consume) falls when moving up the income scale, so does the ratio of tax burden to income.'[15]

Attempts have been made to diminish the regressive effects of a sales tax by introducing differentiating rates. The financial capacity of the taxpayers is taken into account. These different rates do not necessarily disturb economic neutrality. Lower rates applicable to the necessities of life may be defended, since these necessities do not compete with other products: demand is

---

10. Reugebrink, *op. cit.* note 3 *supra*, p. 7.
11. *Idem.*
12. *Idem.*
13. This does not mean that the market mechanism by itself leads to efficient resource use (i.e. produces what consumers want most and does so in the cheapest way). Government regulation or other measures are needed to secure these conditions. Musgrave, *op. cit.* note 9 *supra*, p. 6.
14. *See* W.J. de Langen, *De grondbeginselen van het Nederlands belastingrecht*, Alphen aan de Rijn 1954, p. 234.
15. Musgrave, *op. cit.* note 9 *supra*, p. 443. *See further* on this 'disadvantage' Chapter VI, Section 3.1.

completely inelastic.[16] However, one condition has to be fulfilled: all (similar) necessities of life have to be taxed by the same lower rate. This causes major problems of classification.[17] The result nevertheless remains that the burden on consumption remains regressive.

Differentiation of rates, by means of higher (or luxury) rates, does not distribute the tax burden according to the (supposed) financial capacity of the taxpayer. Given an equal financial capacity, habits in expenditure are too divergent. Therefore differentiating high rates tends to disturb the economic neutrality, without the intended result: the diminishing of the regressivity of the sales tax.

Distribution of the burden of a sales tax by means of differentiation of tariffs has a minimal effect.[18] Therefore economic neutrality is more desirable. This neutrality can best be guaranteed by one, uniform rate. The question of approximation of rates is not only of interest to an internal neutrality, it is also an important issue in the removal of tax frontiers, the subject that will be discussed in part two.

III.2 EXTERNAL NEUTRALITY

The internal neutrality is related to the national aspects of levying a sales tax. The subject of neutrality is also characterized by international aspects, summarized as the external neutrality.

'A sales tax as a general tax on consumption intends to tax the national expenditures of individual consumers. If goods are not consumed in the land of production, while at the same time tax is levied on those goods, this tax is (viewed after the event) unfairly levied, so that a refund should follow on exportation of the goods'.[19]

Further, if it is intended to tax private expenditure, then it should not make any difference whether that expenditure is related to goods produced in the country of consumption or to imported goods. The tax on importation and remission on exportation are called 'tax frontiers'. External neutrality means

---

16. Reugebrink, *op. cit.* note 3 *supra*, p. 19.
17. The classification of what is a necessity and what is a luxury is more in the philosopher's realm than in the tax planner's. Next to this definitional problem, complications arise when goods of a mixed character are involved such as a 'necessity' good in a 'luxury' container. William J. Scott, 'Would Europe's Value Added Tax work for the United States?' *Florida International Law Journal* 1986, p. 110.
18. *See* (for the Netherlands) for example B. de Vet, 'De druk van BTW en accijnzen voor werknemersgezinnen in de periode mei 1974 – april 1975', *Sociale maandstatistiek*, 1978, at 730–737 and R.A. Goudriaan, F.G. van Herwaarden, C.A. de Kam, 'De drukverdeling van omzetbelasting en accijnzen, 1974–1975', E.S.B. 1981, at 128–133.
19. J. Reugebrink, 'The Sixth Directive for the Harmonization of Value Added Tax', C. M. L. Rev. 1978, p. 310.

a neutral functioning of the tax frontiers: the tax on importation is not to exceed the internal tax on like domestic goods; and the rebate on exports has to be the amount that has been actually levied.

In a cumulative cascade tax system the tax burden on a given product cannot be determined exactly. The burden has to be estimated. Under Article 97 of the EEC-Treaty Member States which levy a sales tax calculated on a cumulative cascade tax system may, in the case of internal taxation imposed by them on imported products or of drawback allowed by them on exported products, establish average rates. Application of this article has led to many complaints against policies of 'fiscal dumping and protectionism'.[20]

We will return to the a-neutral aspects of tax frontiers under part two.

Cumulative cascade tax systems not only disturb external neutrality, but also cause a disturbance of competition neutrality.[21] When upon exportation a higher amount is refunded than has actually been levied, one exporter will be favoured above others (who have been confronted with a longer production chain). If the tax on importation is higher than the tax applied to like domestic products, imports will be curbed.[22] The reverse is also possible; when exported goods carry a remnant of the tax burden the exporter will be injured. When imported goods are taxed at a rate that is too low it is detrimental to the domestic industry. It follows that the distortion of competition by fiscal dumping and protectionism, both resulting from cumulative cascade tax systems, led to the conclusion in the European Community that the turnover taxes should be harmonized, as a first step in the direction of elimination of tax frontiers.

20. See K.V. Antal, 'Harmonisatie van de omzetbelasting in de Euro-markt', S. E. W. 1963, p. 12. See further part two, chapter IX.
21. See also Rosendahl, note 7 supra, 'the so-called "competition argument" for border tax adjustments, maintains that such adjustments . . . are necessary . . . to prevent fiscal distortions in competition between domestic and foreign products', p. 91.
22. There is a potential difficulty in clearly identifying a 'like domestic product'. See Rosendahl, note 7 supra, p. 104.

Chapter IV. Systems of Levying a Sales Tax

IV.1 GENERAL

Because a sales tax is a general indirect tax on consumption, two main systems of levying are possible:[1]
   a. Single-stage levies;
   b. Multiple-stage levies.

IV.2 SINGLE STAGE LEVIES

The word 'single' refers to the stage of production or distribution that is covered by the tax. Three sub systems are possible.
   a. a single stage levy at the manufacturer's level (a manufacturer's tax);
   b. a single stage levy at the wholesale level (a wholesale tax);
   c. a single stage levy at the retail level (a retail tax)

IV.2.1 Manufacturer's Tax

Manufacturer's taxes are sometimes called production taxes or business occupation taxes. The single stage manufacturer's tax however, should not be confused with the previously mentioned business occupation tax. The single stage manufacturer's tax is a *system of levying*, the business occupation tax was a matter of legal character. Here we deal with the manufacturer's tax as a system of levying a general indirect tax on consumption. In a manufacturer's tax, tax is only levied on one sector, namely the producers. Dealers (wholesalers and retailers) are not bothered by the system. The special advantage[2] of

---

1. Sections IV.1 till IV.3.2 are to a large extent based on Chapter 3 in J. Reugebrink, *Omzetbelasting*, Deventer 1985.
2. In developing countries sales taxes at the manufacturing level are playing an increasingly important role in their tax systems, due to the growth of free-trade areas among these countries and the replacement of imports of manufactured goods by domestic products. The reason for this important role is that they are the nearest form of sales tax to the customs and

this system of levying is the relatively low number of taxpayers. Thus, perception costs are low. This advantage is overshadowed by disadvantages.

First, production often requires various producers to follow one after the other in the production of a single product. The bakery shop is a manufacturer of bread. Before that grain has been produced, and flour, yeast, sugar, salt, the oven, etc. If all these manufacturers are included in the taxation scheme, the tax will 'pyramid' or cumulate. This means the tax on bread cannot be measured. Also the cumulation of tax creates incentives to restructure business operations either by integration or by transferring functions and costs forward beyond the point of impact of the tax.[3] Some of these distortions can be avoided. It requires, however, complicated legislation.[4]

Second, not all goods are delivered directly from manufacturer to consumers as is the case in a bakery shop. Normally wholesalers and retailers are involved. In order to impose an equal tax burden on identical goods, i.e. in order to guarantee legal neutrality, it is necessary to know the wholesale and retail margin in those cases in which the manufacturer deals directly with consumers. It is to be expected that the manufacturers selling to consumers will charge the same or almost the same prices as the retailer. If the manufacturer is taxed for the full price, the tax burden will be higher than in the case of the 'regular' chain of distribution. In which case part of the price (the wholesale and/or retail margin) is not taxed. In short, the wholesale and retail margin should be deducted from the manufacturers price. But what is the exact margin? Estimates are necessary, or even the introduction of a 'wholesale value' concept[5] risking distortion of competition.[6] All this will not be very

---

excise duties already in operation in those countries and therefore the most likely to be administered successfully. Sales Tax Administration/UN-study, p. 19.

3. Less efficient production and distribution methods combined with higher rates to generate an equivalent amount of revenue are certain consequences of the system. For example, manufacturers may be encouraged to leave to wholesalers certain functions such as transport, warranty and installation which might often be more satisfactorily undertaken by the manufacturers. Sales Tax Administration/UN-study, p. 26.

4. Such as the operation of a so called 'ring system'. Sales by a registered person to another registered person are normally exempt. In order to guarantee that goods are used for productive purposes within the tax-free ring, formal safeguards are required. Sales Tax Administration/UN-study, p. 20.

5. Which implies the use of a 'pure manufacturer's price', i.e. the manufacturers' selling price, exclusive of all expenses of distribution, or else an equalized manufacturers' price based on representative selling prices between manufacturers and wholesalers. See Sales Tax Administration/UN-study p. 24.

6. Also problems may arise in achieving equity between manufactured imports and domestic products. Fully manufactured goods of established brands which are imported by a wholesaler or large retailer often escape the advertising and other selling costs incurred promoting their sales, where the corresponding costs incurred by a domestic manufacturer are included in his taxable amount. Thus a higher rate of sales tax on imports may be justifiable. Sales Tax Administration/UN-study, p. 25.

disadvantageous, as long as the rates are very low. It has been argued that rates up to 2 per cent hardly cause any distortions.[7] Unfortunately there is hardly a state for which such a low rate will suffice.

IV.2.2 Wholesale Tax

Actually the name wholesale tax is incorrect, it would be better to refer to a single stage tax 'preceding the retail stage'. The taxable person is the entrepreneur who delivers to the retailers or to the consumer. Compared with the manufacturers tax the number of taxpayers is higher, the advantage however is that chances of distortion are less. The closer the moment of taxation is to the consumer, the easier it is to calculate the tax as a percentage of the retail price.

The disadvantages of a single stage wholesale tax can be summed up as follows:

1. First, like the manufacturer's tax, the basis of the tax is not the retail price, so identical goods are not necessarily taxed equally, thus legal neutrality is not guaranteed.

2. Second, cases in which manufacturers or wholesalers deliver directly to consumers, require estimation of the retail margin. This estimated margin should be deducted from the tax base. This estimation is rather difficult; there is not one retail price for identical goods. It can be argued moreover that normally the retail margin for luxury goods (like jewelry) is higher than for necessities.[8] This results in a wholesale tax on luxury goods which is lower relatively speaking than tax on first necessities. Of course, this can be solved by various solutions, e.g. rate differentiation. But this will minimize the advantages of the system.

3. Third, a sales tax with a general character cannot permit itself not to cover the services. The difference between goods and services is sometimes rather vague. Within a wholesale tax, however, it is rather difficult to integrate services in the taxation. In order to avoid cumulation deliveries and services are exempt[9] in a wholesale tax, unless deliveries and services are directed towards retailers or consumers. Suppose a house-painter spots a desk behind the windowsill he is painting, the first thing he has to find out is, whether the person who works at the desk is an entrepreneur or not. If so the services of the painter are exempt, provided the entrepreneur is a wholesaler. If not the painter should charge tax!

7. *See* M. Albers, Public Finance Vol. XVI, no. 3/4, 1961, p. 232, as cited by Reugebrink, *op. cit.* note 1 *supra*, p. 29.
8. *Cf.* Sales Tax Administration/UN-study, p. 26.
9. A conditional exemption may be applied, i.e. exemption is conditional on the purchaser's certification that the goods are to be used for wholesale purposes.

-Fourth, as shown above, the field of coverage of a wholesale tax is difficult to define. It is common practice e.g. in Switzerland to make use of registration of entrepreneurs. Transactions between registered entrepreneurs are not taxed. If the purchaser cannot show his registration number, the delivery or service to him is taxed. As a result in Switzerland many retailers registered. This meant that activities towards them remained untaxed, while of course they are taxed for their activities, e.g. to private consumers! Why did they prefer this method? Well, on deliveries by registered entrepreneurs/ wholesalers directly to private consumers a lower rate was applicable than on deliveries to non-registered retailers. If those rates are correctly calculated, retailers will *not* opt for taxation. Nevertheless, it turned out to be more advantageous to opt for taxation. The lesson is that it is extremely difficult to calculate the retail margin in pre-retail sales tax systems. (*See* for an example under IV 4.1.2.)

IV.2.3 Retail Sales Tax

A retail sales tax covers not only the retailers, but all entrepreneurs dealing directly with private consumers. So it is very well possible that a retail sales tax includes manufacturers as well as wholesalers, provided they supply directly to private consumers.

The basis of taxation is the retail price. That is the ideal aspect of this system of levying; in general the tax burden can be calculated exactly. Moreover it does not discriminate between different forms of distribution channels, nor does it give rise to problems of valuation, in contrast to the previously mentioned sales taxes, imposed at earlier stages in the chain of production and distribution. Nevertheless, some disadvantages can be mentioned (especially if the retail sales tax is compared with a VAT). At this place I mention:

a. Taxation takes place at a stage that generally speaking is not economically the strongest. The duty to pay – even when the total tax can be passed forward to the customer – is not without problems: a high standard of bookkeeping is required. Not all retailers are the sort of record keepers upon which a total taxation can rely.

b. Also within a retail sales tax the difficulty is to discern between a taxable and non-taxable delivery. Deliveries to *entrepreneurs* should not be covered by the tax, but how many entrepreneurs do their shopping at retailers? How can it be proven that these deliveries are not to be taxed? Obviously this should be based on statements and bookkeeping. This only adds to the objections put forward under a.

c. A major drawback that a retail sales tax shares with an all stages value added tax (*see* Chapter V *infra*) is the relatively large number of taxpayers

24

which it brings on the taxrolls.

d. Just like in a wholesale tax, in a retail sales tax it is difficult to extend the taxation towards services. The airlines should ask every person who buys a ticket: Do you travel as a private person or as an entrepreneur? Only the travel of private persons should be taxed. Anyone who thinks this objection is exaggerated, I refer to the practices in Norway and Denmark at the time a retail sales tax was levied in these countries. In the beginning services were not included in the sales tax. The result was that often an activity was artificially divided into a service (not taxed) and a delivery of goods (taxed). Separate enterprises were set up to render the services that previously were rendered by the entrepreneur who delivered the goods (in which delivery the service was absorbed); all of this was done to avoid taxation. The Legislator's response to this was to make a whole list of services taxable. The system became too complicated. For this reason, and others, Denmark switched to a value added tax system, *before* the EEC-countries (except France) in which these disadvantages do not exist. (*See* under Chapter VIII.4.)

IV.3 MULTIPLE STAGE LEVIES

In contrast to single stage levies, multiple stage levies cover more than one stage of the production and distribution process.

In cases in which all stages of distribution and production (manufacturer up to and including the retailer) are covered, the tax is referred to as an '*Allfasen Steuer*' (an all-stage tax).

In cases in which not all stages are covered it is referred to as a '*Mehrfasen Steuer*' (a dual-stage tax). As the names show, the theory for these systems of levying originates from Germany. Multiple-stage levies (all and dual stage) can be divided in two groups:
1. Cumulative multiple stage levies;
2. Non-cumulative multiple stage levies.

Multiple cumulative stage levies are often referred to as cascade systems.

IV.3.1 Cumulative Cascade Systems

In an all-stage cumulative cascade system tax is levied in all stages of production and distribution. In a dual-stage cumulative cascade system taxation is restricted to at least two stages (manufacturer and wholesaler, or wholesaler and retailer; it is also possible that the wholesale stage is left out and that taxation is levied in the manufacturing and retail stage). Both in the all-stage and in the dual-stage system the tax is levied over the total price charged.

There are two possibilities:

1. At all stages where tax is levied, the tax rate is the same;
2. At the various stages a different tax rate is applied.

At first sight it may be difficult to believe but the cumulative systems have been very persistent systems in sales taxation. Possibly this is because there is one major advantage of this system: a relatively high yield can be obtained with (a) relatively low tax rate(s). This is, of course, politically an important aspect.

In addition to this, these systems are not complicated from a bookkeeping perspective. In an all-stage system 'simply' a certain percentage of the sales is paid as taxes. Also the whole chain of production and distribution is confronted with an identical burden of administration; nobody can claim to be burdened alone!

Another advantage of cumulative cascade systems is that coverage of services does not create any difficulties. Looking at these advantages one may wonder why these systems have lost appeal in the recent decades. The answer is in one decisive point: the growing importance of the sales taxation as part of the total tax revenue in the various tax systems. The effect being that the rates of sales taxation have gone up constantly. Cumulative cascade systems have advantages only when relatively low rates are applied. When the rates are low, competition is hardly influenced. With relatively high rates, the cumulative cascade system tends to fall apart.

Disadvantages are:

a. The tax is cumulative, the tax burden becomes higher the longer the distance is to the private consumer. The tax can never be (legally) neutral.

b. Cumulation of taxation results in distortion of competition. The longer the distribution or production chain, the higher the tax burden, conversely the shorter the chain the lower is the tax. Integrated businesses therefore experience a lower tax burden than non-integrated (differentiated) businesses. This means that cumulative systems promote integration and cut down on putting work out to contract.

c. Capital intensive businesses are confronted with a higher tax burden than wage intensive businesses. Machines are taxed, wages are not!

d. A major problem is that the external neutrality cannot be guaranteed. The disadvantages of cumulative cascade systems are decisive when rates go up.[10] Various regulations can be used to reduce the disadvantages. The tendency to integrate can be curved down by a so called integration-levy (an internal levy on the internal production or so-called 'self-supply'). The wholesale section with its small margins can be subjected to special rates. Deliveries between manufacturers can be exempt in order to mitigate the tax

---

10. Notwithstanding the objectionable features of cumulative cascade systems when rates go up, cascade taxes have continued in operation for a long time in Europe. Their survival for so long was due to the numerous modifications in the cascade tax, which were carried out in different forms in the various countries. Sales Tax Administration/UN-study, p. 11.

burden. In theory the systems offer many opportunities. At the end they have to be compared with non-cumulative systems.

IV.3.2 Non-Cumulative Systems

These systems, single stage or multiple stage, are all concentrated within a system of value added tax. The character and the technique of these systems will be dealt with at length in the following chapters.

IV.3.3 Synopsis

From the foregoing it follows that multiple stage levies can be divided in
 – cumulative all-stage levies
 – non-cumulative all-stage levies
 – cumulative dual-stage levies
 – non-cumulative dual-stage levies.
The single stage levies, as has been shown under IV.3.1., are quite often cumulative but they can also be made non-cumulative either by various measures or by applying a VAT system.

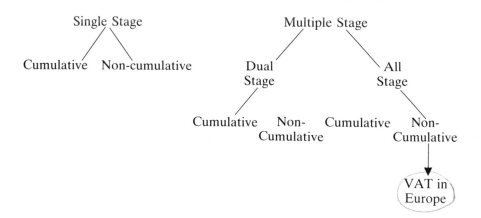

IV.4 EXAMPLES (I)

The following highly stylized examples show a chain of production and distribution of wrapping paper including a forester, a pulp factory, a paper factory, a wholesaler and a retailer. At each stage of production or distribution $1,000 in value (costs/profits) is added, the tax-rate is 10 per cent.

IV.4.1 Single Stage (cumulative) Taxes

IV.4.1.1 Manufacturer's Tax

	Before Tax		Tax		After Tax
Forester	1000	+	100	=	1100
Pulp Factory	2100	+	210	=	2310
Paper Factory	3310	+	331	=	3641
Wholesaler	4641	+	–		4641
Retailer	5641	+	–		5641

Note: In the manufacturer's sector the tax cumulates, the tax burden in the retail sector is still approximately 13 per cent. If the manufacturer's sector integrates, the tax burden will be 300, in the retail sector this will result in a 6 per cent tax burden. Usually tax rates not exceeding 2 per cent in a manufacturer's tax do not cause distortions.[11]

IV.4.1.2 Wholesale Tax

	Before Tax		Tax		After Tax
Forester	1000	+	–	=	1000
Pulp Factory	2000	+	–	=	2000
Paper Factory	3000	+	–	=	3000
Wholesaler	4000	+	400	=	4400
Retailer	5400	+	–	=	5400

Note   The tax burden in the retail sector is approximately 8 per cent. Under the Swiss wholesale tax, see the example mentioned under IV.2.2 apparently the average tax burden in the retail sector was estimated incorrectly based on incorrect calculations regarding the retail margin. Suppose this margin was set at $1500, the tax burden would be approximately 7 per cent, being the rate wholesalers have to charge when selling to private consumers. Evidently retailers prefer to be registered as wholesalers (to whom sales are exempt), in order to be allowed a 7 per cent tax rate.[12]

IV.4.1.3 Retail Sales Tax

	Before Tax		Tax		After Tax
Forester	1000	+	–		1000
Pulp Factory	2000	+	–	=	2000
Paper Factory	3000	+	–	=	3000
Wholesaler	4000	+	–	=	4000
Retailer	5000	+	500	=	5500

Note: Cumulation may only occur when previous sectors buy from retailers and when retailers buy from retailers.

11. Cf. note 7 supra.
12. The actual tax rates involved were 6 and 4 per cent. See Sales Tax Administration/UN-study, p. 29.

IV.5 EXAMPLES (II)

The following examples show the effects of cumulation in multiple stage levies.

IV.5.1 All Stage Tax

	Before Tax		Tax		After Tax
Forester	1000	+	100	=	1100
Pulp Factory	2100	+	210	=	2310
Paper Factory	3310	+	331	=	3641
Wholesaler	4641	+	464	=	5105
Retailer	6105	+	610	=	6715

Note: In each following transaction, tax is also levied over previously paid tax. In this (hypothetical) example the tax burden in the retail sector exceeds 34 per cent, with a tax rate of 10 per cent.

IV.5.2 Dual Stage Taxes

In the first column the manufacturers and wholesalers are taxed, in the second the wholesaler and retailer, in the third, the manufacturers and retailer.

	I			II			III		
Forester	1000	+	100	1000	+	–	1000	+	100
Pulp Factory	2100	+	210	2000	+	–	2100	+	210
Paper Factory	3310	+	331	3000	+	–	3310	+	331
Wholesaler	4641	+	464	4000	+	400	4641	+	–
Retailer	6105 + –	=	6105	5400 + 540 =		5940	5641 + 464 =		6205

Note: A cumulative dual stage tax covering manufacturers and wholesalers is most conceivable, since only a relatively low number of taxpayers are involved. See for the disadvantages Section IV.2.1 and 2.2 supra.

Chapter V. Systems of Levying VAT

V.1 GENERAL

There are several bases for classifying value added taxes. Of particular importance are the extent of vertical coverage through production and distribution stages (the classification that has been used in the previous chapter), the classification based on the treatment of capital equipment, and the method used for calculating tax liability.

V.2 EXTENT OF VERTICAL COVERAGE

When the vertical coverage forward from manufacturing extends through the retail level encompassing all retailers,[1] the VAT can be classified as an all-stage non-cumulative tax. When the tax extends from manufacturing through the last wholesale transaction the VAT may be classified as dual stage non-cumulative tax. When the value added principle is used within the manufacturing section only, with tax applying to each manufacturer on his value added but not to wholesalers or retailers (except to a limited degree), the VAT may be classified as a single stage non-cumulative tax.

V.3 TREATMENT OF CAPITAL EQUIPMENT

Based on the treatment of capital equipment that has been purchased from other firms, there are three separate types of value added tax: consumption type, income type, and product type.

V.3.1 Consumption Type

Under the consumption type value added tax, used in Western Europe, all purchases (with minor exceptions) for use in production (i.e. non-

---

1. The present VAT in the EC countries encompasses only those retailers with sales in excess of certain figures.

consumption), including purchases of durable capital goods, are deductible in calculating a firm's added value. The tax base applies only to the total private consumption. No distinction is made between parts and materials physically incorporated into the product, supplies and fuel, and durable capital goods. Thus the term 'consumption type' is used, the tax is limited to purchases for personal consumption purposes, and if there are no exemptions, the total tax base equals the total personal consumption expenditures. Since all purchases for use in production are deductible, the tax does not penalize capital investment by placing an additional tax burden on capital equipment purchases. Thus the tax is neutral between methods of production since substituting capital for labor (or vice versa) does not affect a firm's total taxes. (The tax would also be neutral between the decision to save or to consume, *see* Chapter VI.1.2.3 *infra*). Since the consumption version is the type of value-added tax used in Europe, there is a tendency to regard this type of VAT as the only type. Because of the aforementioned characteristics I believe it is far superior. After the following short descriptions of the income and product types, we will exclusively deal with the consumption type of value added tax.

V.3.2 Income Type

A second type of VAT is the income type. Under the income type variant of the value added tax, deduction of the VAT on the purchase price of durable capital goods is not permitted in the period of purchase, instead the deduction of an annual depreciation charge arising from such a purchase is allowed. The term 'income type' is given to this version because the total base of this tax is equal to total personal income – for the determination of which the allowed depreciation during the period, rather than the total current outlays on capital equipment is deductible[2] – and therefore equal to the base of personal income tax without exemptions. Obviously this type of value added tax requires the calculation of depreciation. There would be an incentive to classify purchases as current expenditures. Many of the same difficulties arising under an income tax will arise under an income type value added tax.

V.3.3 Product Type

The third type of VAT, the product type, does not allow deduction of VAT on purchases of capital equipment. The result is that capital investments, in

---

2. Even under the consumption type of VAT some characteristics reminiscent of the 'income type' may be found under the treatment of capital goods, in the sense that the immediately deducted VAT is 'followed' for 5 to 10 years in order to ascertain that the proportion of the deducted VAT is still in conformity with the initial use.

effect, are taxed twice, at the time they are purchased and also when the products they produce are sold to consumers.[3] Also a product type of value added tax offers a strong incentive to classify purchases of capital goods as current expenditures. There would be an incentive for self-construction of capital goods. It discriminates against capital intensive methods of production. The product type has been described as a 'tax (that) is best relegated to the realm of conceptual curiosities and should not receive serious consideration in public policy discussions'.[4]

V.4 METHODS OF CALCULATION

Although value added is generally thought of as the difference between the input and the output of a firm, there are three methods for assessing VAT: two of them direct methods, the subtraction and addition methods, and one indirect method, the tax credit method.

Since the tax credit method is so superior to the other methods in terms of application and enforcement,[5] as well as adaptability to various rate modifications, it is now almost universally employed. After a short description of the direct methods, in the remaining chapters the tax credit method will be regarded as the standard method.

V.4.1 The Subtraction and Addition Methods

The subtraction and addition methods involve direct calculation of value added. Under the subtraction method purchases of produced goods and services are subtracted from the figure of sales during a period. At first sight the subtractive method is rather attractive and simple. The major objection to this method is that the final tax burden cannot be calculated when exemptions or rate-differentiations are in use.[6] Each producer or distributor of a certain product can calculate his added value and the tax due based on

---

3. I do not believe that 'thus the full tax burden of capital equipment purchases is absorbed by the business purchaser and is not passed on to the consumer'. If this were so, cumulative sales taxes are non-existent. Contra William J. Scott, 'Would Europe's Value Added Tax Work for the United States', *Florida International Law Journal* 1986, p. 107.
4. Tax Reform For Fairness, Simplicity, and Economic Growth – The Treasury Department report to the President, Volume 3. Value Added Tax, Office of the Secretary, Department of the Treasury, November 1984, reprinted in Commerce Clearing House Vol. 71 no. 56, 27 December 1984 (hereinafter Treasury report) at 6.
5. One may add that VAT is also a sophisticated tax. Once it has been introduced it should yield optimally its advantages, especially regarding neutrality.
6. J. Reugebrink, *Omzetbelasting*, Deventer 1985, p. 56.

the applicable rate. The tax burden on the final product, however, is not certain. In other words, there is no relation between tax rate and final price. Thus the method conflicts with the 'general' aspect of the legal character of the tax. Also neither internal nor external neutrality can be guaranteed.

The addition method involves the addition of the sum of all the elements that constitute value added wages, rent, royalties, interest, profit and the like. Since profit normally reflects a capital depreciation allowance, the method is probably suitable[7] for an income type of value added tax and not for a consumption type.[8] So far as is known, this addition approach has only been utilized in Michigan.[9]

V.4.2 The Tax Credit Method

The tax credit, or invoice, method is almost universally used for assessing VAT. Under this method a firm's tax liability is calculated by allowing the firm to subtract value added tax paid on the purchases from tax due on its sales. Thus value added, as such, is never calculated at all (but the effect is exactly the same as if the figure were calculated). Three major advantages may be attributed to the credit method.[10]

First, this method is (almost) universally used in other countries.

Second, the other forms of calculating almost of necessity require the use of an annual tax-paying period, rather than a monthly or quarterly basis feasible in the tax credit method.[11]

Third, the tax credit method makes an important contribution to enforcement of the value added tax, but also can be used by taxing authorities for income purposes.[12] As an example let us use the same figures as in Chapter IV.

7. Or 'inextricably intertwined' Charles E. McLure, 'Thoughts on A Value Added Tax', *Tax Notes*, 23 October 1979, p. 540.
8. It shares many of the problems of income taxation, where interjurisdictional transactions are concerned. The addition method is not suited to destination-principle taxation. Charles E. McLure, 'State and Federal Relations in the Taxation of Value Added', *The Journal of Corporation Law* 1980, p. 130.
9. John F. Due, 'Economics of the Value Added Tax', *The Journal of Corporation Law* 1980, p. 63.
10. Due, *op. cit.* note 9 *supra*, p. 63.
11. It would seem that even shorter periods are possible as suggested by E. Souley and G. Brannon, 'Direct Consumption Taxes: Value Added and Retail Sales', in *Tax Policy: New Directions and Possibilities*, Washington 1984.
12. *See* A. Pedone, 'Italy', p. 205, in H. Aaron (ed), *VAT Experiences of some European Countries*, Deventer 1982. In this context the VAT was considered an 'anathema', since evasion was considered more difficult. *Cf.* D.J. Puchala and C.F. Lankowsky. 'The Politics of Fiscal Harmonization in the European Communities', *Journal of Common Market Studies* 1977, at 176.

V.4.3 Example Tax Credit Method

	Sales	Tax on Sales	to Treasury
Forester	1000	100	100
Pulp Factory	2000	200	200 − 100 = 100
Paper Factory	3000	300	300 − 200 = 100
Wholesaler	4000	400	400 − 300 = 100
Retailer	5000	500	500 − 400 = 100
			500

Note: In a period of only purchases and no sales the tax declaration will be negative, the tax paid on purchases should be remitted. In case of a consumer-strike the treasury will be left empty handed. (*See also* Chapter VI Section 4.5.)

V.5 SUMMARY

Value added taxes can be classified based on the extent of vertical coverage, on treatment of capital equipment, and on the methods used for calculation. In the remainder we will deal exclusively with an all stage non-cumulative value added tax, of a consumption type, calculated by the tax credit method.

Chapter VI. The VAT as Fiscal Phenomenon

VI.1 INTRODUCTION[1]

Although the VAT cannot possibly be eliminated from West-European countries, within the national tax systems its place is disputed even more than its counterpart: the income tax. This is mainly caused by its inability to reduce inequalities in wealth and income in view of its regressive or, more or less, proportional distributional patterns, particularly at high income levels. It is useful to survey the disadvantages and advantages attributed to the VAT, as a general tax on consumption.

VI.2 ADVANTAGES

The value added tax offers several advantages. The following are presented in an arbitrary sequence.

VI.2(1) Fiscal Advantages

The coverage of the VAT as general tax on consumption is rather extensive. Each person willing to continue his existence will be reached by the tax, even when he or she does not enjoy an income or possesses any wealth. This can be looked upon as a negative aspect, we will return to this later, but from a purely 'fiscal' perspective,[2] it should be noted that even a relatively low rate will yield a relatively high revenue (as compared to a retail sales tax, generally restricted to the delivery of goods).

Moreover, the tax can spread its burden over the widest possible range of goods and services, and so make avoidance less possible, or at least less

---

1. Parts of this chapter have been heavily drawn upon J. Reugebrink, *Omzetbelasting*, Deventer 1985, Chapters 2 and 6.
2. I.e. the sole purpose is to raise revenue.

'painful' for the Treasury,[3] than with specific commodity or excise taxes which may be affected by the availability of non-taxable substitutes.[4]

Another 'fiscal' advantage is the fact that it is rather (too) easy to raise the VAT rate(s) if additional revenue is needed.[5] Also VAT is a less fluctuating source of revenue.

Consumption may be affected by a change of economic conditions, but it is more likely that wages, profits and other income are much more volatile. The yield of VAT therefore will be more independent of recessionary or expansionary fluctuations than income tax.

The relatively high yield is coupled with rather low perception costs.[6] The VAT's relative self-enforcement is believed to minimize abuse and is one of the tax's attractive features. Under the invoice credit VAT, the tax is considered to be largely self-policing.[7] The tax is collected by entrepreneurs – a relatively small group – who have to collect the tax themselves. The revenue agency's task is merely a controlling one.

VI.2.2 Psychological Advantages

The rather high yield of a VAT can be reached in a fairly painless, or at least an almost unnoticed, way. VAT, at least in Europe, is hidden in the price, based on the tradition of concealing (sales) taxes. By some this concealment of the taxes is seen as a great advantage; it avoids confrontation with the tax and minimizes popular resistance, particularly in the (frequent) cases when the rates go up.

Notwithstanding the European tradition, one may object to the psychological advantage that a tax can be collected virtually unnoticed by the persons who are supposed to carry the burden. The credit method necessitates separation of the tax element from the price on all transactions among taxable persons. The question is whether the separate quotation rule is also required

---

3. Since generally the input tax will not be deducted, thus only the tax on added value will be avoided.
4. And the yield from which may diminish through a change in fashion or in social customs. Sales Tax Administration/UN-study, p. 3.
5. Reagan believes that the VAT gives the federal government too much power because of it being easy to raise VAT-rates, this made him a formidable opponent against the introduction of the VAT in the US. *N. Y. Times*, 22 February 1985, at 10, col. 6. cited in William J. Scott, 'Would Europe's Value Added Tax Work for the United States?', *Florida International Law Journal* 1986, p. 117.
6. Although the indirect perception costs, carried by the taxable persons, i.e. entrepreneurs, are not to be underestimated.
7. D.B. Spizer: 'Comments, The Value Added Tax and Other Proposed Tax Reforms: A critical Assessment', *Tulsa Law Review* 1979, p. 203. *See also* note 3, *supra*. However, the European experience with VAT has proven that the VAT is not entirely free of tax evasion.

on the sale to the final consumer. There are various arguments in favor of this.[8]

First, a seller will frequently not know whether a purchaser is buying for business (production) or consumption purposes. If on all invoices the tax is separately quoted, there is no need to delineate between the different use, from a seller's point of view.

Second, one may argue that as a matter of principle, tax payers should know the amount of tax they are paying; in order to keep them aware of and interested in the (optimal) ways the tax revenues are spent by the government.[9] Indeed, one may wonder whether in these modern times it is still acceptable that tax payers are treated as being 'under age' by purposely concealing the tax burden. Of course, one may counter this by arguing that the 'veiling' effect of the VAT in no way affects the 'nonage' or 'majority' of modern tax payers.[10] They will have a sufficient sense of realism to recognize the inclusion of the tax in the purchase price. From this point of view concealment of the tax is simply an effort to minimize the pain.

A third argument in favor of separate quotations is that the likelihood of a full shift of tax is increased. Moreover, concealment of the tax at the retail level may complicate the task of the retailer in calculating his tax liability, especially when various rates are used, since the retailer must factor out the amount of the tax due from his gross receipts.[11]

VI.2.3 Economic Advantages

Unlike an income tax, a VAT is neutral toward the saving- consumption choice. In a VAT-system, let us say with a single rate of 20 per cent, the decision to save will, in the next year, lead to a spending power of the saving plus interest. For example, 100 + 10 per cent interest; both will be taxed at the moment of spending, resulting in a spending power of 88 and a tax of 22.

In an income tax system (with the same rate) the decision to save will lead to taxation in the year of saving, 20 out of 100; the next year the lower interest (compared to the previous example) will also be taxed, 1.6 out of 8, resulting in a spending power of 86.4 instead of 88 in a VAT-system. This example only shows that VAT is neutral with regard to the choice between consumption now (100 minus 20 per cent) or later (110 minus 20 per cent), since the net return on saving is not affected by value added tax.[12] A VAT is believed to be

8. John F. Due, 'Economics of the Value Added Tax', *The Journal of Corporation Law* 1980, p. 64.
9. *See in general* J. Reugebrink, *Omzetbelasting*, Deventer 1985, p. 15.
10. J. Verburg, *Tussen de regels door*, Deventer 1973, p. 9.
11. The validity of this argument depends on the degree of sophistication in registration. For smaller entrepreneurs estimates on the gross inputs may be more convenient.

superior to an income tax in fostering capital formation (and economic growth).[13] A second economic advantage that is attributed to VAT is its possibility to be used as an instrument to influence production and consumption. A tax may be used, by varying its rates, in a conscious effort to offset economic fluctuations; that is, the rates can be raised to counteract tendencies toward overheating of the economy and reduced to mitigate recessionary tendencies.

The efficiency of the value added tax above other tax instruments to influence consumption and production is not at all clear. A temporary *increase* of the value added tax could be expected to exert a greater dampening effect upon the economy than a temporary increase in income tax. For it is the income tax that is more likely than VAT to be paid out of savings rather than consumption, and quite probably the income tax will be collected later. More importantly some expenditures might be postponed until VAT returned to its normal rates. The other side of the coin, however, is that expectations of a counter cyclical increase in the VAT rate could induce anticipatory buying that would have perverse macroeconomic effects.[14] One may also wonder whether *lowering* of VAT rates, in times of depression, will lead to an increase in demand. One should not be too optimistic. It seems clear that prices will go down, given a lower demand, when rates are reduced. The question is how long the lower prices will hold out? One cannot rule out that prices will return to previous levels. Under these circumstances reintroduction of the regular VAT-rates will result in an additional inflatory effect. An example of this is the Dutch experience of the introduction of an exemption of turnover tax on textiles in 1955. This exemption served as a compensation for a rent increase. Initially the exemption indeed resulted in a favorable effect on the housekeeping budget. A short while later the textile producers decided that the exemption was also meant to profit them. The greater demand following from the price reductions was used to increase the prices to approximately the previous level. Now two parties regret this: the housewives and the Revenue; with prices eventually unchanged, the yield of the turn over taxes had dropped![15]

---

12. However, McDaniel points out that young people and the elderly are typical dissavers, so they would bear a heavier tax burden under the VAT relative to income, as an illustration that value added tax proposals to increase savings cannot be accepted uncritically. Paul R. McDaniel, 'A Value Added Tax for the United States? Some preliminary reflections', *The Journal of Corporation Law* 1980, p. 22.

13. *Cf.* Scott, *op. cit.* note 5 *supra*, p. 113. As to the question whether VAT is inherently inflationary, depending on the degree of changing other taxes, or replacing another form of sales taxation, introduction of a VAT will probably result in a one-time price increase but not necessarily in a continuing price spiral.

14. Charles E. McClure, 'Economic Effects of Taxing Value Added', in *Broad-Based Taxes*, Richard A. Musgrave (ed), Baltimore 1973, p. 183.

15. H. Kahmann, 'Niederländische Umsatzsteuerreformen und ihre volks– und finanzwissen–

Finally, it is frequently argued that value added tax improves the trade balance. This argument is primarily based on the realization that VAT can be rebated on exports and levied on imports. Although the favorable effects are not at all clear, the argument is used by those who favor the introduction of a VAT, as was done recently in Japan where the proposals were voted down by the *Diet*. Since this attributed advantage forms one of the pivots in the dispute on border adjustments it will be dealt with under Part Two.

VI.3 DISADVANTAGES

The disadvantages that are attributed to VAT may be summarized as follows: VAT is a regressive tax, it taxes lower incomes more heavily, therefore, it is an 'a-social' tax.

VI.3.1 VAT a Regressive Tax?

VAT is considered to be regressive 'since the ratio of consumption to income (the average propensity to consume) falls when moving up the income scale, so does the ratio of tax burden to income.'[16] One may wonder whether the ratio of tax burden to income is the most relevant factor; shouldn't it be replaced by the ratio of tax burden to expenditures? I believe this is true for a tax system that more heavily relies upon expenditure taxes.[17] But since the VAT generally is introduced as a complementary of the income tax, it is most useful to apply the same starting point to both taxes in order to be able to discuss the tax burden of both taxes.[18] It should be clear that a VAT, in which one rate is applied, will be regressive based on the ratio of tax burden to income.[19]

Moreover, the regressive nature of the value added tax has two facets: the absolute burden of the tax on those below the poverty level and the regressive

---

schaftlichen Auswirkungen' (Finanz Archiv, NF 17) cited by J. Reugebrink, *Omzetbelasting*, Deventer 1985, p. 17.

16. R.A. and P.B. Musgrave, *Public Finance in Theory and Practice*, New York 1976, p. 443.

17. *Cf.* Reugebrink, *op. cit.* note 1 *supra*, p. 17.

18. This does not alter the assumption that the VAT is a consumption related tax. Description of the tax as a production tax is not helpful either and only confuses the issues. Due, *op. cit.* note 8 *supra*, p. 63. Ture, however, still argues that the VAT should be regarded as a tax whose burden is distributed in relation to capital and labor income. Norman B. Ture, 'The Basic Economics of a United States VAT', *The Journal of Corporation Law* 1980, p. 53.

19. However the regressivity of a particular tax should not be viewed as a fatal flaw in any system. George N. Carlson, 'Value Added Tax: Appraisal and Outlook', *The Journal of Corporation Law* 1980, p. 42.

effect for those above the poverty level.[20] We will return to that after this.

Various methods are available at least theoretically to reduce the regressivity, to make the VAT proportional or perhaps progressive.[21]

In general, two measures are applied to influence the regressivity: one is the introduction of exemptions and/or reduced (or even zero) rates; the second is the introduction of higher (or luxury) rates. Both techniques are commonly applied, although many objections can be raised, since differentiations in rates and exemptions unduly complicate the technique of levying VAT.[22] Before we turn to this aspect under Section VI.4 (we will return to the question of a uniform rate under part two) some observations have to be made on the poverty level mentioned earlier. Generally speaking differentiation of rates is not a desirable means of alleviating regressivity. Whether reduced rates are applied or not, it is still possible that for the lowest incomes the VAT is an excessive burden.[23] In that case the VAT should be offset by a refundable tax credit administered through the income tax system or by increased transfer payments.[24]

20. Treasury report, p. 43.
21. At least four alternatives exist for reducing the burden of the tax on the lower income individuals and families and to lessening the regressivity of the tax: 1. Adjustment of government transfer prices; 2. Zero-rating (or reduced-rating) of food and other necessities; 3. Provisions of a refundable credit and 4. The personal exemption value added tax. Treasury report, p. 43 and Chapter 8, pp. 87–107.
22. Besides a single rate VAT is easiest and cheapest to administer. The techniques of rate-differentiation or exemptions 'pollute' the system. During a recently held International Symposium organized by the French Ministry of Finance in association with the Committee on Fiscal Affairs of the OECD the following was mentioned on consumption taxation in relation to taxation of low incomes: 'though a few participants remained convinced that such products as basic foods and medicines should be exempt or taxed at lower rates than such products as televisions and jewelry, most of those present saw no role for consumption taxes in alleviating poverty or redistributing income. Several participants supported a single-rate VAT on as wide a base as was possible in practice – as recently enacted in New Zealand – it being considered that the multi-rate systems existing in most OECD countries were the result of past legacies, political difficulties and voters' misunderstandings. In favor of single-rate broad based taxes it was argued that in industrialized countries, consumption patterns between rich and poor were not very different, so that multi-rate taxes were unlikely much to increase progressivity and that multi-rate general consumption taxes had a built–in drawback both for governments' collection and traders' compliance costs, which hardly justified the slight progression to which they might contribute,' OECD, Taxation in Developed Countries, Paris 1987, p. 43.
23. According to McDaniel (op. cit. note 12 supra, p. 21) it appears likely that the introduction of tax preferences into the VAT will not be controllable, and that the income tax will be further riddled by tax expenditures to alleviate problems seen created by the VAT, or that both will occur.
24. In the US this refundable credit is presently utilized by six of the states that impose retail sales taxes. These six states are Colorado, Hawaii, Idaho, Massachusetts, Nebraska and Vermont. Carlson, op. cit. note 19 supra, at 42. He recognizes that many individuals do not appear on any income tax return and that it is important that these individuals be brought within the scope of the tax credit.

Neither are luxury rates an effective instrument to alleviate regressivity, as mentioned earlier (under Chapter III.2) habits in expenditure are too divergent. It suffices to conclude that the preferable way to reduce the regressive effects of VAT is to offset the effects by adjusting the income tax rates.[25]

VI.4 SOME IDIOSYNCRASIES OF THE VAT

'The VAT is a paradox: (using the credit method) the VAT is a tax in which those who believe themselves exempt are taxed, and those who believe themselves taxed, are generally exempt. This is not valid at the retail level; a retailer who is believed exempt is nevertheless taxed, and indeed taxed, when subject to taxation. Whoever grasps the meaning of this, will not have any trouble understanding VAT.'[26]

VI.4.1 Scope of the VAT

VAT, as levied in Europe, covers all stages of production and distribution. Also, the services supplied by taxable persons are taxed. The deduction of input tax prevents cumulation. It is the purchaser of the goods or services who decides whether – and to what extent – the tax is deductible. The problem of the house-painter under IV.2.2, who had to verify the status of his client regarding the taxability of his service, is solved under VAT, since the owner of the building decides whether the tax is deductible; a decision that will be scrutinized by tax auditors later! In other words under VAT part of the burden of proof regarding the tax-liability is transferred to the taxpayer. This strong characteristic of the VAT will be discussed in part two, when VAT will be compared with the retail sales tax.

In the example under V.4.2, VAT was applied in a series of transactions within one tax period. In practice, transactions will not always follow this smooth example. Sometime tax has to be paid over a period in which no invoices were received so no deductions can be claimed, or sales will be low and purchases high resulting in a refund of tax. From this, the following may be concluded regarding the scope of VAT.

25. The emphasis on regressivity, in my view, should at least be neutralized by viewing it in the context of an overall economic scheme, one regressive element does not necessarily create a regressive system (*Cf.* Carlson, *op. cit. supra* note 19, p. 42). Whatever additional purposes a tax system may have, to me the most important goal seems to be to raise money efficiently; a single rate VAT appears to be the most effective and the least expensive to operate. The employment of different rates, however successfully this may have been done in Europe, takes its tolls in lost capital and efficiency.
26. J. Reugebrink, *op. cit.* note 1 *supra*, p. 58.

a. The name tax on value added is rather misleading, when the invoice method is used. In a given tax period the value added may not be taxed. Whatever has been purchased in a tax period is not necessarily sold in the same period, as a matter of fact it may take a while before the purchased goods will be sold. Nevertheless, the input tax shown on the invoices in that period is deducted.

b. The tax may be deducted *immediately*, meaning the moment it is charged on an invoice. That moment is quite probably before the goods have been resold, but it is also possible that the moment of deduction is even before the actual payment of the bill.

c. All tax charged by suppliers can be deducted to the extent the goods and services are used for the purposes of taxable transactions. Thus the tax is deductible on intermediate goods, capital investments, services, imports, stock, etc.

d. The name value added tax only refers to a method of calculation. The 'real' value added is only taxed if a company is considered between its 'birth and death'. Basically the VAT, using the invoice method, is only a method to discern between productive and consumptive use. The former should not be taxed, hence the deduction of input tax, the latter should be taxed, hence the exclusion of deduction. The attribution of goods and services to either use cannot be made by the supplier, because he does not know the purchaser's intentions. For that reason the tax is proportioned to its use by the purchaser of the supplies, he is the only one who can calculate which route the goods and services will take.

VI.4.2 VAT is Not a Cost-Price Factor

Within the chain of production and distribution VAT does not influence the price of goods or services.[27] Whatever tax the one entrepreneur is charging, the other will deduct it, at the same moment. Therefore, entrepreneurs within the chain of production and distribution calculate in net-figures; VAT does not raise the cost-price. It is a suspense account. Put differently, the entrepreneur does not only purchase goods and services, he also purchases a claim on the Revenue, that diminishes his (future) tax debt. The most essential record is the invoice, which must list the VAT paid, so business purchasers are able to claim credit for VAT already paid by preceding business sellers.[28] It is possible that, in a given period, the deduction claimed exceeds the tax due. In particular this will happen in case of big investments, then the difference will be refunded to the tax payer. This is known as a VAT without 'butoir'. A

---

27. Unless exemptions are applied, *see* Section VI.4.4 *infra*.
28. This facilitates calculation of the tax and also provides a *clear audit trail*. Due, *op. cit.* note 8 *supra*, pp. 63–64.

butoir is a doorstop (or buffer) that was used on carriages, preventing the opening door from 'going too far'. In France it was believed (and still is) that one 'goes too far' by refunding the tax. It is, as such, conceivable that deduction is limited to the tax amount due.[29] The (not yet) deducted tax would be qualified for deduction in the tax period to come. Generally this limitation of the right to deduct – referred to as the 'buffer-rule' – is not applied in VAT-systems. In certain situations the immediately deductible tax results in refunds, safeguarding an optimal neutrality.

VI.4.3 The 'Recouping Effect'

As previously has been discussed the value of the claim on the revenue, given by an entrepreneur to his purchaser, is, in the end, decisive of the amount the purchaser has to pay to the Treasury. In other words an entrepreneur, who is taxed at a lower rate than his client, will only transfer a lower claim. The result is that the purchaser will have to pay 'more'.

Example:

in a given tax-period, A purchases the following:

merchandise	10 000	VAT	10%	=	1000
services	4 000	VAT	10%	=	400
electricity	1 000	VAT	5%	=	50
			input VAT		1450

In the same period A sells for 20 000; the applicable VAT-rate is 10 per cent and the VAT due on the sales is 2000. Since A may deduct 1450, 550 is payable in taxes. The total input was 15 000, thus it may be concluded that the value added was 20 000 minus 15 000 = 5000. Therefore the tax should have been 10 per cent over 5000 = 500. In reality, 550 had to be paid.

The fact that A experiences a raise in payable tax is caused by the tax rate applicable to the electricity, namely 5 per cent instead of 10 per cent. The amount the electricity company paid less, A will have to pay more. This phenomenon is called the 'recouping effect'. From this effect it follows that the rate at the last stage of the distribution chain is decisive of the tax burden. Lower rates applied in previous stages have no effect whatsoever nor do higher rates.[30]

---

29. Except for entrepreneurs, that exclusively are engaged in export-activities.
30. In other words: the rate applied to the final domestic sale (to consumer or for export) dictates the aggregate tax burden on the sale, regardless of the rates applied at earlier stages. Charles E. McLure, 'State and Federal relations in the taxation of Value Added', *The Journal of Corporation Law* 1980, p. 128.

VI.4.4 Exemptions

When an exemption is applied, the 'recouping effect' will occur too. But exemptions have yet another consequence. The input tax that may be attributed to the exempt supply cannot be deducted (this being the major difference between exemptions and zero-rates, the latter leaving the right to deduct unimpaired). Thus an exemption, somewhere in the chain of production or distribution, causes cumulation. Suppose in the example under V.4.3 the pulp factory is exempt.[31] Therefore it cannot deduct the input tax and does not have to pay any tax either. The paper factory will not be able to deduct any VAT, since the pulp factory was exempt. The result is a cumulation of tax,[32] as the following example will show.

	Sales	Tax on sales	to Treasury
Forester	1000	100	100
Pulp factory	2100	exempt	–
Paper factory	3100	310	310
Wholesaler	4100	410	410 % 310 = 100
Retailer	5100	510	510 % 410 = 100
			Total 610

It may be clear that the pulp factory is exempt, but actually taxed! The cost-price of its product has gone up by 10 per cent and in the next stages this nondeductible tax is part of the tax base. Therefore the tax burden is not 500 + 100, but 500 + 100 + 10; the 10 being cumulated tax on the non-deducted tax.[33]

It is evident that a much more effective or attractive exemption would be an exemption combined with the right to a deduction. When the VAT was introduced in Europe apparently the defenders of a consequent application of the system could not prove wrong the others like France, where the exemptions without deduction were already applied. The result is not only that an element sneaked into the system disturbing its functioning as a strictly neutral tax, more importantly the VAT is to a great extent burdened with rules that are difficult to apply in practice. For example, it is very possible that an entrepreneur purchases goods and services both for exempt and taxable purposes. The result is that the input tax has to be segregated between the part attributable to exempt activities and the part attributable to taxed

---

31. In practice not a subject, a taxable person, will be exempt from taxation, but certain taxable transactions are exempt i.e. the delivery of pulp.
32. It is assumed that neither the pulp factory nor one of the next stages is willing, or forced by market mechanisms, to bear a tax penalty.
33. Thus pressure is built into the system to keep it relatively free of exemptions. Cf. McDaniel, *op. cit.* note 12 *supra*, p. 26.

activities. These so-called *pro-rata* rules have formed a major source of disputes between taxpayers and the Revenue.

An additional complication is the tendency of exempt entrepreneurs toward internal production. The nondeductible tax on parts will be lower than the tax on a finished product, the difference being the wage component related to the manufacturing of the finished product. In order to avoid distortion of competition, a levy on the internal production of exempt entrepreneurs is necessary. The result of this can be that the internal levy overshoots a possible purpose of the exemption, (or at least an attractive aspect from the collecting point of view) to exclude from taxation a particular group of entrepreneurs!

VI.4.5 Exemption at the Retail Level

For entrepreneurs dealing with private consumers it all works out differently. A lower rate at the retail level is indeed effective, since the purchaser cannot deduct it. Also an exemption in the last stage can be useful: the result of the exemption is that the 'added value' in the last stage is not taxed, generally resulting in a moderation of the tax burden. This, however, is not a plea to exempt the retail level altogether; many reasons can be given to include the retail level in the taxation.

a. Exempting the retail level would mean a distortion of (legal) neutrality, since the margins in retailing not only differ as per product, but also as per company.

b. Many entrepreneurs purchase their products at the retail level. Exempting the retail level would put the retailers out of the business of selling to entrepeneurs, because the retailer cannot transfer a claim on the revenue, resulting in cumulation.

c. In many cases the retail level cannot be distinguished. Quite often the manufacturer supplies the private consumer, while at the same time his products are sold by separate retailers. Consequently separate retail margins should be applied. As mentioned earlier these can hardly be calculated.

d. Obviously higher tax rates are necessary to guarantee the same yield as when retailers are included.

VI.4.6 Consequences of the Deduction Mechanism

The consequences of the right to deduct the input tax may be summarized as follows.

a. Within a chain of distribution or production VAT does not influence the cost-price of a product or service, provided no exemptions are granted. The VAT is merely an expense account.

b. The result of the immediate deduction of input tax is that investments, stock, etc. are at the entrepreneur's disposal *tax free*, since the tax has been deducted right at the moment it has been charged.

c. A lower or higher rate only has effect when applied at the end of the distribution chain i.e. when a product or service enters the consumer's sphere. Before that, the recouping effect occurs.

d. Exemptions are only effective at the end of the chain. However, their effect is not an exemption, but a moderation of the tax burden, because the input tax cannot be deducted. An exemption in a previous stage only disturbs neutrality and results in a higher tax burden.

e. Generally (i.e. when no exemptions are applied) the deduction results in a tax burden that is capable of exact calculation at any moment in time. Thus the external neutrality is optimally guaranteed.

f. Also internally the tax is neutral. Since the tax burden is independent of the length of the production or distribution chain. The recouping effect results in an equal tax burden for integrated as well as differentiated businesses.

g. The burden of VAT is eventually carried by those who are not entitled to deduct the tax. Mostly these will be consumers. Although complete forward-shifting can never be guaranteed by the legislator, the deduction mechanism insures that the shifting should not cause too many problems in any industrial branch.

h. *A VAT, that includes the retail stage, is conceptually not different from a single levy at the retail stage*, assuming the (neutrality distorting) disadvantages of such a single stage levy are avoided.[34] In each tax period the revenue receives a yield equal to the rate applicable to the sales at the retail level during the period given.

One should realize that in the stages previous to the retail stage, a cycle has taken place of payments and deductions, a series of transactions that would have shown a circular course, resulting in nothing, if at the retail level nothing had been sold. In the tax period concerned all entrepreneurs have paid their taxes due. It may be that some have enjoyed a refund, but by far most will have handed over tax money. The sum of all these payments, however, is equal to the tax rate applicable to the retail sales in the given tax period.

The conceptual equality of the VAT with a retail sales tax does not make the two systems of taxation exchangeable. Before we turn to the superiority of the VAT over the retail sales tax in chapter thirteen the European VAT and its flaws will be discussed.

34. VAT is simply a method of collecting a retail sales tax through a withholding system *cf.* Due, *op. cit.* note 8 *supra*, p. 63 and McDaniel, *op. cit.* note 12 *supra*, p. 16. However, some issues like the question whether a business purchase should be exempted from the tax because the item is used for business purposes is generally more easily resolved in a VAT. These, however, are tax collection issues not substantive tax base issues. McDaniel, p. 18. Both VAT and a retail sales tax (RST) address the retail stage of the production-distribution sequence, RST by definition, VAT by design. S. Cnossen, 'VAT and RST: A Comparison', *Canadian Tax Journal* 1986, p. 567.

Part Two

Coordination

of

Value Added Taxes

in

The European Community

Chapter VII. Background of Common VAT; The Customs Union

VII.1 INTRODUCTION

'Determined to lay the foundations of an ever closer union among the peoples of Europe, and recognizing that the removal of existing obstacles calls for concerted action in order to guarantee steady expansion, balanced trade and fair competition.'[1] Belgium, France, Germany, Italy, Luxembourg and the Netherlands signed a Treaty in Rome on 25 March 1957 establishing the European Economic Community (EEC). At the same time the Treaty establishing the European Atomic Energy Community (Euratom) was signed,[2] whereas as early as 1951 the Treaty Instituting the European Coal and Steel Community (ECSC)[3] had entered into force. Since 1978 these Communities have been referred to as the Community.[4] By accession treaties

1. First and third consideration, preamble Treaty Establishing the European Economic Community 294–297 U.N.T.S.17, (authentic languages: French, German, Italian and Dutch).
2. Treaty Establishing the European Atomic Energy Community, 294–297 U.N.T.S. 259.
3. Treaty Instituting the Coal and Steel Community, 18 Apr. 1951 261 U.N.T.S. 140.
4. In 1965 the so-called Merger Treaty established a Single Council and a Single Commission of the European Communities, 8 Apr. 1965, J.O. 1967, C 152. In accordance with European Parliament's decision on a single designation for the Community, (O.J. 1978, C 63) the terms "European Community" or "Community" serve as the collective designation for the grouping constituted by the Member States and for all the institutions created by the treaties establishing the European Community. Four primary institutions are established by the EEC-Treaty, the Court of Justice, the European Commission, the Council of Ministers and the European Parliament. The *Court of Justice* ensures that in the interpretation and application of the Treaty the law is observed. The *Commission* consists of 17 members, who are appointed by the governments of the Member States by common accord and who are chosen for their independence. The commission's primary function is to propose legislation. The European *Parliament* consists of 508 members elected by direct universal suffrage. The Parliament has no true legislative power, its advisory and supervisory powers include the power to censure the Commission and the ability to amend the Community budget. The *Council* of Ministers consists of a delegation from each Member State at the ministerial level and a delegation from the Commission. The Council's primary function is to enact legislation. It also has primary budgetary responsibilities.
There are various types of Community legislation (article 189 EEC-Treaty): A *regulation*

Denmark, Ireland and the United Kingdom joined the Community on 1 January 1973.[5] While the Norwegians decided to stay out,[6] Greece acceded at the beginning of 1981.[7] With the entry of Portugal and Spain[8] on January 1986, the Community has 12 Member States.[9] The aims of the Community include: the creation of a single integrated (common) market freed of restrictions on the movement of goods and services and capital, and freed of obstacles to freedom of movement for persons; the abolition of obstacles to the right of establishment of businesses and employment; and the institution of a system ensuring that competition is not distorted. Clearly these goals have a number of consequences for, among other things, the tax systems of the Member States, in particular the abolition of national customs duties and the harmonization of the sales taxes and other major indirect taxes. These consequences can best be viewed from the historic perspective of the creation of the European customs union.

VII.2 THE CUSTOMS UNION

Article 2 of the EEC-Treaty states the economic and political objectives of the Community. The promotion throughout the Community of a harmonious development of economic activities, a continuous and balanced expansion, an increase in stability and an accelerated raising of the standard of living are the dynamically defined economic objectives. The political objective is a closer relation between the Member States. The two means for achieving these objectives are the establishment of a common market and the progressive approximation of the economic policies of the Member States.

The philosophy behind these principles may be summed up as 'the larger the market and the keener the competition, the better'. A larger market is reached by the establishment of a common market, 'the meeting place of the supply and demand from all the Member States, without discrimination by

---

shall have general application. It shall be binding in its entirety and directly applicable in all Member States.

A *directive* shall be binding, as to the result to be achieved, upon each Member State to which it is addressed, but shall leave to the national authorities the choice of form and methods. *Recommendations* and *opinions* shall have no binding force.

5. Acts relating to these accessions, O.J. 1972, L73.
6. Council decision adjusting the instruments concerning the accession of non Member States O.J. 1973, L2.
7. Documents concerning the Accession of the Hellenic Republic O.J. 1979, L291.
8. Documents concerning the accession of the Kingdom of Spain and the Portuguese Republic O.J. 1985, L302.
9. Encompassing some 320 million people and generating a combined gross domestic product of European Currency Units (ECU) of 2800 billion in 1983. In comparison, the United States had 235 million inhabitants in that year and its GNP was ECU 3600 billion *See* S. Cnossen, 'Tax Coordination in the European Community', *Tax Notes* 18 May 1987 p. 692.

the Member States among the participants in the market on grounds of nationality or any other distortion of competition.'[10]

Article 9 of the EEC-Treaty provides that the Community will be based upon a customs union,[11] covering all trade in goods including the prohibition of customs duties between Member States on imports and exports and all charges having equivalent effect and the adoption of a common customs tariff in their relations with third countries. The provisions of the customs union shall apply to the products originating in Member States and to products coming from third-countries which are in free circulation in the Member States. It is remarkable that the Treaty does not define a customs union. To be distinguished are[12] a tariff-community, a free-trade association, a customs union and an economic union. In a *tariff-community* the participating countries have one common tariff valid against third-countries while import duties on imported goods from the Member States are, at least to a large extent, abandoned.

In a *free-trade association* there is no common tariff of import duties; only goods *originating* from the Member States are not subjected to import duties. A *customs union* comprises a tariff-community; in addition, the whole customs legislation has been harmonized; also the other taxes due on importation are harmonized. In an *economic union* a customs union is accompanied by free movement of persons, services and capital. In an economic union a common commercial policy is defined, and the union acts as a unity in the mentioned areas. The given definitions are promulgated by the Study-group for a European Customs Union of the OEEC;[13] they do not cover the customs union in the EEC-Treaty; since the Treaty does not prescribe that the whole customs legislation is to be harmonized.

Although a customs union is not defined in the EEC-Treaty, Article 3 mentions a range of items involved in the establishment of a common market, which come under the definition of an economic union. Even if it is assumed that harmonization of the customs legislation is not a legal requirement for a customs union and that a common commercial policy falls under an economic union, both are nevertheless essential to achieve the objective of the EEC. A common market cannot exist when customs duties are imposed between the participants in the market. A common outer tariff prevents distortion of

---

10. P.J.G. Kapteyn and P Verloren van Themaat, *Introduction to the Law of the European Communities*, Deventer 1973, p. 53.
11. *See* 'Commission de la Communauté Economique Européenne *v.* Gouvernement de La Republique Italienne', C.M.L. Rev. 1961, p. 39. (Lagrange, Advoc. Gen.) (la communauté "est *d'abord* une union douanière") (the community "is *in the first place* a customs union") (emphasis is original) quoted in John P. Stigi III, 'The Elimination of European Community Border Formalities', Va. J. of Int'l L. 1987, p. 369.
12. J. Reugebrink, *Aan de grens,* Deventer 1978, p. 41.
13. E.W. Meijers, *De Europese Economische Integratie*, Leiden 1958, Annex I.

competition between the members and the deflection of the flow of trade. A common customs tariff, however, may not be uniformly applied. Specific rules governing the basis of assessment in application of the tariff are required to prevent manipulation. Equal application of the common tariff can be disturbed by deferred payment of customs charges. More than mere harmonization of these aspects is necessary to attain equal treatment of all participants in the market, a necessary aspect of freedom of trade. In order to avoid artificial diversions of trade patterns, a common commercial policy should also be defined. Furthermore, harmonization is necessary because of the 'own resources decision'.[14] All importers have become European taxpayers. Equality of taxation demands equal application.[15]

The customs union is the foundation of the Community. One of the benefits of a customs union is optimal distribution of work. The producer with the lowest costs of production obtains, apart from distortion of competition, the same market opportunities in all Member States as local producers with higher costs of production. A customs union leads to enlargement of the scale and the growth of production of the most efficient enterprises in the union.[16] In order to establish and then maintain the customs union various steps have to be taken:[17]

1. Customs duties and similar charges on trade between Member States must be abolished.
2. A common outer tariff has to be established.
3. Quantitative restrictions and measures having equivalent effect between Member States have to be eliminated.
4. A whole range of supportive legislative provisions is necessary for the application of a common customs tariff and a common commercial policy has to be adopted as a matter of community policy.
5. Provisions must be made in respect of internal taxation, in particular the taxes which influence the movement of goods between the Member States.

VII.3 ABOLISHMENT OF CUSTOMS DUTIES BETWEEN MEMBER STATES

Articles 12 through 17 of the EEC-Treaty provide for the abolition of customs duties and similar charges. Article 12 provides that Member States shall refrain from introducing between themselves any new customs duties on

---

14. *See* Section VIII.5.1 *infra.*
15. *Cf.* Section II.2 *supra.*
16. Kapteyn/Verloren, *op. cit.* note 10 *supra*, p. 54.
17. I have here drawn freely upon my article on 'Introduction to Customs Law', published in L.I.E.I. 1981, pp. 77–105.

imports or exports or any charges having equivalent effect and that they shall refrain from increasing those charges which they already apply in their trade with each other. The text of Article 12 sets forth a clear and unconditional prohibition of the introduction of new customs duties. According to the spirit, arrangement and wording of the EEC-Treaty, Article 12 must be interpreted as having direct effects and as giving rise to individual rights which the national courts must safeguard.[18] Articles 13, 14 and 15 of the EEC-Treaty call for the progressive elimination of customs duties on imports during the transitional period and the progressive elimination of charges having an effect equivalent to customs duties on import. Article 16 calls for the abolition of customs duties and charges having equivalent effect on exports by the end of the first stage.

The procedure for the gradual abolition of customs duties on imports and the abolition of export duties is of historical interest only. In general it did not involve great difficulty most probably because there were no difficulties in the qualification. The customs duties were included under such denomination in the national lists of tariffs.[19] The qualification of 'charges of equivalent effect' is more difficult.[20] The requirement for the progressive abolition of these charges is a logical and necessary complement to the first paragraph of Article 13, which calls for the elimination of customs duties. The concept of charges with equivalent effect has been interpreted in the light of the objects and purposes of the Treaty, particularly the provisions dealing with the free movement of goods. A special charge on gingerbread within the framework of a market organization in the rye industry,[21] charges on export of art treasures to maintain the national collection,[22] a charge on imported diamonds to benefit the Diamond Workers Social Fund[23] and charges levied for sanitary and other inspections performed to protect public health[24] have been classified as charges having the equivalent effect of customs duties. The Court of the EEC concluded that 'any pecuniary charge, however small and whatever its destination and mode of application, which is imposed unilaterally on domestic or foreign goods by reason of the fact that they cross a frontier, and which is not a customs duty in the strict sense, constitutes a charge having equivalent effect within the meaning of Articles 9, 12, 13 and 16 of the Treaty, even if it is not imposed for the benefit of the State, is not discriminatory or protective in effect and if the product on which the charge is imposed is not in competition with any domestic product.'[25] Any conceivable

18. Case 26/62, Van Gend en Loos (1963) E.C.R., 12.
19. A tariff is a list of names of products, the nomenclature, and the duties set forth.
20. R. Barendts, 'Charges of equivalent effect to custom duties', C.M.L. Rev. 1978, P. 420.
21. Case 2 and 362, Gingerbread (1962), E.C.R., 425.
22. Case 7/68, Art Treasures (1968), E.C.R., 423.
23. Case 2 and 3/69, Diamond Workers (1969), E.C.R., 211.
24. Case 29/72, Marinex (1972) E.C.R., 89.
25. Case 24/68, Statistical Levy (1969), E.C.R., 201.

pecuniary charge imposed on importation or exportation may be affected by this broad prohibition.

On several occasions the argument was made that the charge is a consideration for services rendered and not a charge having the equivalent effect of a customs duty. A 'fee' to defray the costs of compiling statistical data,[26] a levy for compulsory health and sanitary inspections to offset the costs incurred[27] and a small charge imposed on exports of fruits and vegetables to cover expenses relating to quality control at the national frontier and a national mark for the exportation granted when specific requirements as to the quality had been met[28] have been held as charges of equivalent effect. The Court of the EEC has not flatly rejected the consideration for services argument because a charge for a specific individualizable service actually rendered which does not exceed the actual cost of the service will not be classified as a charge of equivalent effect. Concrete applications that meet these conditions are difficult to find.[29] Only charges for sanitary inspections were held not to be charges of equivalent effect.[30] These cases, connected with Community rules and international treaties on inspection, constituted a clear break with precedent.[31] The Court reasoned that the obstacles to intra-Community trade were less than in the situation prior to the introduction of the community rule or the treaty concerned.[32]

General exceptions to the prohibition of charges of equivalent effect are the permissions by specific Treaty provisions.[33] This reservation is necessary in particular in view of the Articles 95 through 99 of the EEC-Treaty, the provisions on internal taxation of imported products. We will return to this subject under Section VII.7.

VII.4 COMMON OUTER TARIFF

A customs union requires a common outer tariff. Articles 18 through 29 of the EEC-Treaty call for the establishment of a common customs tariff (CCT) to be applied in its entirety upon the expiration of the transitional period set forth in the Treaty. Essentially four different customs tariffs[34] had to be

---

26. *Idem.*
27. Case 29/72, Marinex (1972), E.C.R., 89.
28. 63/74, Cadskey (1975), E.C.R., 281.
29. The maintenance of the reputation of the fruit and vegetable products was considered insufficient ground to assess the personal benefit for each exporter.
30. Case 46/76, Bauhaus 1977, E.C.R., 5. Case 89/76, Commission vs. the Netherlands (1977), E.C.R., 1355.
31. *See* Barends, note 19 *supra*, p. 434.
32. *Idem.*
33. Case 24/68, Statistical Levy (1969), E.C.R., 201.
34. In the Benelux one customs tariff has already been applied.

combined into one common tariff based on the Brussels Nomenclature,[35] with an acceptable amount of sub-headings. The level of the duties in the common tariff was initially fixed at the level of the arithmetical average of the duties in force on 1 January 1957. Exceptions to this rule were made with regard to items shown in various lists added to the Treaty. Drawing up of the CCT was extremely difficult. For example the Benelux-countries used subheadings to impose a tariff on plastics[36] based on the form of appearance (blocks, plates, powder); other countries imposed a tariff based on the type (polyethylene, polyvinylchloride). Starting with five subheadings based on form and ten based on type leads to fifty subheadings. The initial effort resulted in a tariff with over 20,000 sub-headings. After revision the subheadings numbered about 10,000. A special team of customs experts managed to reduce the list to less than 3,000 common items, 2,809 to be exact.[37] In accordance with Article 28 of the EEC-Treaty the Council may decide on alterations or suspensions of tariffs within certain limits. Usually these regulations are published in December.

Starting 1 January 1988 the CCT based on the Brussels Nomenclature is replaced by a Community tariff based on the Harmonized Commodity Description and Coding System, a single harmonized method of classifying goods for customs, statistical and trade purposes, that is adopted by all the major trading nations, including the United States and Japan. At the same time the Community Integrated Tariff, the TARIC is introduced.[38]

VII.5 QUANTITATIVE RESTRICTIONS

Establishment of a customs union requires the abolition of quantitative restrictions as between the Member States. If this obstacle were not removed, all other measures taken to establish a customs union would be nullified. The protection afforded by customs duties or other charges could simply be replaced by a quota system or other quantitative restrictions. Quantitative restrictions include all legislative or administrative rules or administrative measures restricting the importation or exportation of one or more products

---

35. Based on the Convention on the Nomenclature for the Classification of Goods in Customs Tariffs, Convention of 15 December 1950, concluded at Brussels.
36. See H. de Pagter, 'Een aantal aspecten van het tarief van invoerrechten', I.U.N. 1975, p. 352.
37. Regulation 950/68. O.J. 68, L172.
38. The result will be a Tariff Trade Code Number of up to eleven digits for each separate description of goods identified in the tariff. Of these, the first six digits will be the Harmonized System code. Other digits will be required for Community and national statistical purposes and the balance will be used to identify the particular tariff treatment and customs regime which may apply to each description of goods. See G. Darracot, 'The Customs Union', Taxation, 26 September 1986, p. 505.

according to quantitative norms or value.[39] Articles 30 through 35 of the EEC-Treaty prohibit quantitative restrictions and all measures having an 'equivalent effect'. It is very difficult to decide what are measures of equivalent effect. The Commission has issued a statement that in its opinion measures having equivalent effect cover 'all legislative and administrative provisions as well as administrative practices forming a barrier to imports that might take place in the absence of such provisions or practices, including those provisions and practices which render imports more difficult or expensive in comparison with the sale of the home product'.[40] All measures which do *not equally* affect domestic and imported products, such as measures prescribing less favorable prices for imported than domestic products, or determining profit margins are covered.[41] Trade regulations equally affecting imported and domestic products are considered measures with equivalent effect if their impact on the free movement of goods is more restrictive within the framework of the regulations. Some persons assert that discriminatory and non-discriminatory measures are permissible outside the scope of the exceptions provided for in Article 36 whenever the measures are needed to achieve a legitimate purpose. Others express the opinion that all measures which constitute an obstacle to free movement of goods, except those falling within the scope of Article 36, should be prohibited.[42] The Court of Justice takes the *general* position that under Article 30 and Article 36 'All trading rules enacted by Member States which are capable of hindering directly or indirectly, actually or potentially intra-Community trade are to be considered as measures having an effect equivalent to quantitative restrictions.[43] Furthermore 'In order to be able to rely upon Article 36, the Member States must remain within the limits provided by that provision as regards the objective to be reached and the nature of the means'.[44]

As can be seen from the preceding, only a strict application of the rules can set up a customs union. In addition to the framework formed by the abolishment of customs duties and quantitative restrictions between the Member States, and by the institution of a common outer tariff – supporting legislative provisions are necessary to guarantee the continuity of a customs union.

VII.6 SUPPORTIVE LEGISLATIVE PROVISIONS AND EXTERNAL COMMERCIAL POLICY

The customs union of the Community is supported by legislative provisions

39. Derrick Wyat and Alan Dashwood, *The Substantive Law of the EEC*, London 1980. p. 97.
40. J.O. 1970, L 13/29.
41. W. Van Gerven, 'The recent case law of the Court of Justice concerning Articles 30 and 36 of the EEC-Treaty', C.M.L. Rev. 1977, p. 7.
42. *Idem*, p. 8.
43. Case 8/74, Dassonville (1974), E.C.R., 837.
44. Case 7/68, Art Treasures (1968), E.C.R., 629.

designed to ensure uniform application of rules throughout the Community. These provisions can be reduced to three types: tariff supporting legislation, specific tariff legislation and formal legislative procedures. Once a customs union is established the reduction of discrepancies between the national commercial policies of the Member States is essential. Autonomous national commercial policy measures may result in a deflection of trade into those countries with least restrictive regimes.

VII.6.1 Tariff Supporting Legislation

The uniform application of tariff measures can only be guaranteed if rules that are susceptible to varied interpretation are clarified. We will only deal with the rules regarding the type of goods and the customs valuation.

The *classification of goods* may present problems. One item may be capable of classification under various headings, especially when assortments of goods are imported.[45] The rule is that the classification follows from the good from which the essential character is derived. The general rules of classification and the interpretative notes – appearing at the head of each section and chapter of the Tariff – are not sufficient to eliminate all possibilities of divergent interpretation by national administrations. To ensure uniform application supportive legislation has been issued in Regulation 97/69, which established i.a. a Committee on nomenclature to examine nomenclature questions.[46] Each year technological developments cause numerous new classification problems. Therefore classifications criteria and the interpretative notes are constantly updated.

Customs duties may be assessed upon the value of the goods, *ad valorem* duties, or on a specific standard, such as weight or volume, or by a combination of these methods. Ad valorem duties are considered more equitable because all items, inexpensive and expensive, are taxed in equal proportion. Specific duties tax inexpensive items more heavily. Ad valorem duties readily adapt to monetary fluctuations and to international comparison. Specific duties are easy to levy and difficult to evade. In inflationary periods ad valorem duties are more advantageous to the Revenue.[47]

Without regulation of the *valuation of goods*, tariff-changes may be agreed

---

45. Consider classification of a plastic drawing box, containing a ruler, a pair of compasses, a slide rule, a pencil and a pencil sharpener. In this case the essential character is derived from the ruler!
46. The procedure is that the Commission can only rule on a nomenclature issue if a consenting opinion has been given by the Committee. If no opinion or a negative opinion is given, the Commission must submit a proposal to the Council, which must then make a decision within a given time limit on the basis of the proposal. If no Council decision is forthcoming the power of the Commission becomes operative again and the Commission rules.
47. Only a few specific duties still exist in the Community Tariff.

upon without effect. The transaction price may be ignored and arbitrary values substituted. Regulation of valuation prevents disguised re-introduction of higher or lower tariffs. Article VII of the GATT[48] calls for the 'actual value' as the basis for assessment of the customs valuation. Two different concepts are possible, the theoretical and the positive. The theoretical concept employs the 'normal price', the price which the goods would fetch at the time of the valuation in a sale in the open market between buyer and seller independent of each other. Generally the invoice is accepted as the basis for assessment when the positive concept is used. In the theoretical valuation, a range of factors are taken into account: community of interest (a sale between related persons), intercompany-pricing, responsibility for warranty, advertisement, marketing, royalties and licences affect the 'normal' price. The theoretical concept was used in Regulation 803/68, issued in 1968 by the Council of the E.E.C.[49] In general, theoretical valuation in the EEC usually exceeded positive valuation. It was considered protectionistic by the Americans, as they do not subscribe to the theoretical definition of customs valuation. Continuous interference with intercompany-pricing resulted in a trade-barrier between the Community and the United States. The Community revised its views in order to liberalize world trade. The developing countries find a positive conception objectionable since customs duties still form an important source of income and the stricter positive rules give less chance for manipulation. Ultimately, a uniform positive definition has been introduced during the Tokyo-round, the agreement on implementation of article VII of the General Agreement on Tariffs and Trade.

In the new definition[50] customs valuation of imported goods is the *transaction value*, the price actually paid for the goods when sold for export to the country of importation. Six methods are available to determine the transaction value. The transaction value of imported goods, identical goods, or similar goods may be used. Alternatively the retrograde method (based on the unit price sold in the greatest aggregate quantity), the computed value or the 'global method' (the determination by reasonable means) are available. The essential difference between the new definition and Regulation 803/68 is that warranty, advertisement and marketing no longer form a part of the assessment of value. In case of a community of interests the transaction value will be accepted if the importer proves that the value closely approximates the transaction value in sales to unrelated buyers. The agreement on implementation of article VII of the General Agreement on Tariffs and Trade was to become effective on 1 January 1981, however, the Community and the United States agreed to an effective date of 1 July 1980. The content of the agreement

48. *See* Chapter IX, *infra*.
49. J.O. 1968, L148.
50. *See* H. de Pagter and R. van Raan, *Customs Valuation*, Deventer 1981.

has been issued as Regulation 1284/80,[51] to prevent discussion about direct application of the agreement within the Member States. This Regulation sets up a regulatory committee,[52] the Committee on Valuation, that may examine any question concerning the application of the valuation regulation.

VII.6.2 Specific Tariff Legislation

The three Community Treaties provide for a sectorial policy for coal, steel, atomic energy, transport and agriculture. Tariff measures are deemed to be necessary in the agricultural sector to protect the agricultural sector in the Community against the low world-market price level. Import levies are charged to bridge the gap between Community prices and the world-market prices. Refunds are granted for exports. Specific tariff regulations, apart from tariff regulations resulting from the sectorial policy, are based on the association and preferential (*see* Section 6.4 *infra*) agreements or on autonomous decisions. The Council of the EEC may, by virtue of Article 28, decide on *suspensions*. When there is – or threatens to be – a shortage of a certain product within the Community specific tariffs may be suspended. Duties in the Customs Tariff can be subjected to a *quota-system*. Common tariff quotas, are based on Article 28 of the EEC-treaty. The institution of tariff-quotas is permitted under Article XIII of the GATT provided that the principle of non-discrimination is maintained. Generally the quotas have to be open globally; however, if a quota is allocated among supplying countries, the allocation is to be based on proportions supplied during a previous period.

Regulations and directives are issued concerning the *exemption of customs charges* pursuant to Article 28 or 100 of the EEC-Treaty. Exemptions are granted for various reasons. Idealistic, social or cultural motives may underlie the decision to admit goods free of customs charges. Some exemptions are based on economic and commercial considerations. Community rules are required to prevent a deflection of trade to the Member States whose regime of exemptions is least restrictive. Additionally, Community rules are required because the proceeds from customs duties form one of the Community's own resources.[53] It would be inappropriate if a single Member State could autonomously decide to lower these resources.

VII.6.3 Formal Legislative Provisions

Settlement of customs charges varied to a large extent in the various Member States. It was feared that different payment facilities would cause a deflection

---

51. O.J. 1980, L134.
52. *See* for the procedure, note 45 *supra*.
53. *See* Chapter VIII.5.1 *infra*.

of trade and receipts in customs charges. Directives have been issued, wherein entitlement to *deferred payment* is considered a right for importers in all Member States. The period for payment is fixed at thirty days. If a Member State grants additional time for payment it should be done on financial terms equivalent to those prevailing on the national money markets. Since the 'own resources decision' fear of deflection of receipts in customs charges is unfounded; all these receipts form one of the Communities own resources. Still, deflection of trade is to be avoided by uniform payment facilities.

The *customs clearance operations* to which importers were subjected differed largely from one State to another. Additionally, the time-lapse between the arrival of the goods in the territory and the assignment of a customs regime differed substantially. The possibility of deflection of trade and receipts of customs charges made it necessary to establish a few essential principles to guarantee uniform application. The key principle is that all goods arriving in the customs territory have to be placed under customs supervision. A summary declaration is required for the identification of the goods. The goods may be placed in temporary storage in premises under customs supervision. The maximum period allowed for such storage is 15 days. After this period the assignment of a customs regime or transit or customs clearance is required. Apart from the customs regime of inward processing, allowing a conditional exemption from duties during the period of the processing operation, the goods can be assigned to other customs regimes namely the regime of bonded warehouses or the Free Zone regime.

The regime of bonded warehouses enables the goods to be stored under customs supervision in a place designated for that purpose while the collection is suspended. The advantages of suspension on the collection of duties play an important role at the time of importation when the necessary documents are not yet available or when the importer simply wants to delay payment for economic reasons. It is possible that the definite destination is unknown. In expectation of one of the destinations (transit, assignment of a customs regime or customs clearance) the goods may remain free of duties in a bonded warehouse for a maximum period of five years. The goods must be declared to the customs officials. Goods in bond may undergo 'usual handling'.

A *Free Zone* is any territorial enclave set up with a view to ensuring that goods in that Zone are regarded as not being in the customs territory of the Community for the purposes of application of customs duties, agricultural levies, quantitative restrictions or any charge or measure of equivalent effect. The Free Zone regime can be regarded as an expanded warehouse regime. Goods in a Free Zone may undergo 'usual handling'. Retention of goods in the Free Zones is not subjected to time restrictions. Although goods in Free Zones are regarded as being outside the customs territory, these goods are under control of the customs organization of the territory in which the Free Zone is located. Treatment of goods other than for 'usual handling' must be in conformity with the general rules applicable to inward processing. Consumption and utilization other than 'usual handling' can only take place in the Free Zone under the conditions imposed in other parts of the customs territory. In short, consumption requires customs clearance. The reduction of formalities during *Community transit* is an important achievement in the formal regulations. The introduction of a customs union and a common outer tariff does not create the obligation to clear goods at the point of entrance into the customs territory. There are advantages to clearing goods at the place of destination provided the delays 'en route' caused by frontier stops are reduced to a minimum. Widespread establishment of internal customs offices facilitates a more rational distribution of staff. Checks and controls carried out near the enterprises or on their premises are more efficient and rapid. The rotation schedule of transportation can be improved by avoiding immobilization at frontiers. In intra-Community trade the destination principle applicable to indirect taxation requires checking the movement of goods between Member States. The Community transit system established two procedures. The first procedure applies generally to goods which are not in free circulation, while the second applies to goods which are in free circulation. The external procedure for goods from third-countries on which duties have not been paid or for which the customs formalities have not been fulfilled can be illustrated by the following example.

Suppose goods from the United States, not yet in free circulation, are to be transported between Rotterdam and Florence via Belgium and France. In Rotterdam a 'T1'declaration is made at the customs office, since 1 January 1988 the so-called single Administrative Document is used. The office will register the 'T1' declaration and prescribe the period within which the goods must be produced at the requisite office in Florence. Identification of the goods will generally be secured by sealing. Transit through Belgium and France will be accomplished simply by presentation of the 'T1' declaration at the customs office of passage mentioned in the declaration and customs inspection to ensure that the seals are not broken. Upon arrival the goods are presented to the customs office in Florence within the specified time limit. After the necessary checks have been made a copy of the document is forwarded to the departure office in Rotterdam. If within a certain period of time this copy is not received in Rotterdam an inquiry is made at the customs office of passage in Belgium and France. This makes it possible to determine irregularities. The procedure is similar for internal Community transit, except that no customs duties are paid. The transit operation requires a guarantee bond be given by the declarant. The Community transit regime permits goods to move within the Community under a single procedure regardless of the number of internal frontiers crossed.

VII.6.4 External Commercial Policy

Once a customs union is established the reduction of discrepancies between the national commercial policies of the Member States is essential. Autonomous national commercial policy measures may result in a deflection of trade to the countries whose regimes are least restrictive. Without a common commercial policy other common customs measures are threatened. Deflections of trade and economic difficulties may result in a progressive appeal to safeguard measures, which would interfere with the free circulation of goods. A common commercial policy may be seen as the key of customs law in the Community. The progressive establishment of a common commercial policy is provided for in Article 3 and Articles 110 through 116 of the EEC-Treaty. The subject of the common commercial policy is too extensive to be treated here in detail.[54] Only certain aspects of the common commercial policy like the trade agreements concluded by the Community will be illustrated.

The common commercial policy embraces the measures intended to regulate economic relations with third countries including the movement of goods and the rendition of services and payments therefore. At the heart of the common commercial policy are the *associations*, free trade and preferential trade agreements. Associations as a preliminary to membership of the EEC must be distinguished from associations formed for development assistance.[55] Only European countries qualify for an association as a preliminary to membership of the EEC. Such an association has been formed with Greece and Turkey. In the case of Greece this resulted in accession to the Community on 1 January 1981. The associations as a special form of development assistance have developed historically from the associations with the overseas countries and territories. This was continued after the territories had become independent in the Conventions of Yaounde and Arusha. The accession to the Community of three new members in 1973 caused a growth in the candidates for association. With then 42 African, Carribean and Pacific States the Convention of Lome was concluded on 28 February 1975. Although based on the EEC-Treaty as such, the politically sensitive term association was not used. Several times the convention has been amended and ameliorated.

The basis of the Convention is not mutual free import between the Community and the ACP-States. These countries only agreed not to discriminate between Member States and to apply the most-favoured national rule to the Member States of the Community. The Community in return grants free entrance of products originating from the ACP-countries excepting only a

---

54. *See generally* E.L.M. Völker and J. Steenbergen (eds.), *Leading cases and materials on the external Relations Law of the EC*, Deventer 1985.
55. *See* Kapteyn/Verloren, *op. cit.* note 10 *supra*, p. 486.

number of agricultural products. In order to stabilize the revenues from exportation of a series of basic products, such as cocoa, coffee, cotton, the *Stabex* is introduced as a financial mechanism to prevent fluctuations in export revenues. Fluctuations in world market prices or quantities can have serious financial repercussions in states dependent on the export of one or few commodities.[56] The Convention also provides for financial and technical cooperation.

Preferential trade agreements have been concluded with the EFTA-members that did not wish to become members of the Community for political or economic reasons. Finally trade-agreements granting preferential treatment have been concluded with Mediterranean countries. Some of these trade agreements bear the character of an association but for formal reasons this term has been avoided. In the case of Malta and Cyprus the trade agreements have brought about customs-unions with the Community without formal membership.

VII.7 INTERNAL TAXATION

In addition to all the previously mentioned measures the Treaty calls for regulation of internal taxes that influence intra-Community trade. As a matter of fact, regulation of these taxes is as essential to the creation of a customs union as all other earlier mentioned provisions. This is because internal commodity taxes have the potential to hinder international trade as effectively as customs duties and non-tariff barriers in the field of customs-law. Normal import duties discriminate against imported products.[57] They produce revenue but essentially they are imposed to protect the home-produced products. *Customs duties of a fiscal nature* are duties on products that are not produced in the country levying the tax. These duties are like normal customs duties in that they are charged exclusively on imported goods. They are distinguishable in that they are designed solely to produce revenue. Article 17 of the EEC-Treaty calls for the abolition of customs duties of a fiscal nature, but the Member States retain the right to substitute an internal tax which complies with the provisions of Article 95 of the EEC-Treaty governing internal indirect taxes. A turnover tax, a general tax on consumption, and other specific consumer taxes such as excises are examples of permissible internal indirect taxes. It is permissible to impose an indirect tax on imported products if there are no similar home-produced products. However, an internal indirect tax may not afford indirect protection to other domestic products which can be used for the same purpose. A

---

56. *Idem*, p. 491.
57. *See* J. Reugebrink, *Aan de grens*, Deventer 1978, p. 22.

consumption tax is permitted only if the home production, if any, is also taxed. The Court of Justice of the EEC has frequently affirmed this prohibition of fiscal discrimination. For example, France's imposition of a tax on Scotch whiskey in excess of that imposed on domestically produced Cognac was deemed a prohibited fiscal discrimination.[58] The fiscal nondiscrimination provision of Article 95 of the EEC-Treaty is having direct effect.

The EEC-Treaty prohibits any refund of an internal tax on exportation to the territory of any Member State exceeding that actually imposed internally.[59] Such a repayment would equal an export-subsidy. This provision creates problems with a cumulative cascade tax system. As has been discussed under chapter IV supra in a cumulative cascade system tax is imposed on several or all stages of production and distribution. At each stage the tax is cumulated. Vertical and horizontal integration of production or distribution results in a reduction of taxes under the cumulative cascade system. The tax burden on a given product cannot be determined exactly because a product may have different producers with varying levels of integration and therefore carry different tax burdens. Consequently this burden has to be estimated. This estimation affects the external neutrality. Initially, average rates on imported products or refunds on exported products were allowed by Article 97 of the EEC-Treaty regarding internal taxes.[60] Although this article has lost its practical importance since the adoption of directives concerning harmonization of turnover taxes the average rates in a multi-stage system demonstrate the possibility of manipulation in the form of disguised protective levies or export-subsidies.

Two initial turnover tax directives[61] obliged the Member States to harmonize their laws concerning turnover tax. The objective of the directives was replacement of cumulative multi-stage systems with the system of *tax on added value*. This VAT is neutral since the tax on input is credited against the tax due on the output. The extent of vertical or horizontal integration of production or distribution does not affect the tax ultimately imposed. Therefore, the external neutrality is also guaranteed since the levy upon importation and the remittance upon exportation equal exactly the internally imposed tax.[62] We will now turn to the harmonization of the turnover taxes in the following chapter.

---

58. Case 168/78 Commission *vs.* France E.C.R., 347.
59. Article 95, EEC-Treaty; compare with Article III, GATT *see* Chapter IX *infra*.
60. *See further* Chapter IX *infra*.
61. *See further* Chapter VIII Section 3 *infra*.
62. Specific taxes on consumption, *excises*, like general taxes on consumption also require the principle of the country of destination and tax frontiers. Excises in the Community have not been noticeably harmonized to date. Harmonization of the turn over taxes has usurped other harmonization efforts causing a delay in harmonization of excises. The White Paper, however, offers proposals for an all-over harmonization. *See* Chapter XI *infra*.

Chapter VIII. Harmonization of Turnover Taxes in the EC

VIII.1 INTRODUCTION

The value added tax is not a new phenomenon. Wilhelm von Siemens is often[1] credited with first proposing the tax for Germany in 1919, under the name 'Veredelte Umsatzsteuer', an 'ennobled turnover tax'.[2] As early as 1921 Thomas S. Adams suggested it in the form of a business taxation, as a substitute for the US corporate income tax.[3] Initially the suggestions of both writers yielded little influence. However, from time to time tax authorities referred to the ideas of Adams and von Siemens. In these references a remarkable aspect is that in Anglo-Saxon countries the VAT-system was considered as a system of levying business-taxation in conformity with Adams; on the European continent the system was approached consistently as an 'ennobled turnover tax.'[4] A clear example of this different approach is the synchronous introduction, namely in 1953, of a BAT, a business activities tax, in Michigan, a direct business occupation tax levied based on a VAT-system and of a VAT in the same year when France introduced the TVA, 'taxe sur la valeur ajoutée'.

The real growth of acceptance of the value added tax stems from the formation of the European Economic Community. We will turn now to the introduction of VAT in Europe.

---

1. Lindholm claims that the first proponents to advocate the value added tax in the US date back as early as 1911. The much greater acceptance of VAT in Europe than in the US is attributed partially in response to the 'exportation' efforts of American economists and partially as a result of independent experimentation and initiative. In this scenario von Siemens (see note 2) is not even mentioned. *Cf.* Richard W. Lindholm, 'The origin of the value added tax', 6 *Journal of Corporation Law* 1980, no. 1, pp. 11–13.
2. Wilhelm von Siemens, *Veredelte Umsatzsteuer*, Siemensstadt 1919.
3. Thomas S. Adams, 'Fundamental Problems of Federal Income Taxation', *Quarterly Journal of Economics*, Vol. 35, no. 4, 1921, p. 553, *et. seq.*
4. *See* J. Reugebrink, *Omzetbelasting*, Deventer 1985, p. 54.

VIII.2 PRELUDE

Article 99 of the EEC-Treaty instructed the EEC-Commission to consider 'how the legislation of the various Member States concerning turnover taxes, excise duties and other forms of indirect taxation, including countervailing measures applicable to trade between Member States can be harmonized in the interest of the common market.'[5] In 1960 the Commission responded to this instruction by appointing three working groups. Working group I, specially charged with the task of researching the possibilities of harmonizing the turnover taxes in the EEC, appointed again three study groups: subgroups A, B, and C composed of experts from the Member States and the Commission.[6] The findings of these working groups were published as the so-called ABC-report.[7] Also in 1960, the Commission appointed the Fiscal and Financial Committee to study the extent to which the tax systems of the Member States conflicted with the establishment of a common market.[8] The conclusions of the ABC-report and the report of the Fiscal and Financial Commitee are in substance concordant (although the reports are differently structured). Both recommend that the Member States abolish the cascade tax and *adopt the value added tax* in its place.[9] The report of the Fiscal and Financial Committee, chaired by Professor Fritz Neumark from Germany[10] (hence, generally referred to as the Neumark-report) summarized the defects of the cascade turnover tax as follows: 'It causes distortion of competition within the national economics where it is applied and artificially promotes the concentration of enterprises, but, in addition, it distorts the international trade regulations because of the impossibility of calculating exactly the overall charge of

---

5. From this wording conclusions may be drawn regarding the legal character: it is evident that the turnover taxes are considered 'indirect' taxes (see 'and other forms of indirect taxation'), also the turnover taxes are apparently treated as taxes having the same legal character, notwithstanding the extreme differences in systems of levying, since the Treaty only prescribes 'harmonization'.
6. To sub-group A was referred the question of the possibility of the removal of tax frontiers and the need for physical inspections at borders to administer the system of border tax adjustments in relation to turnover taxes. Sub-group B was given the task of considering the adoption of a common single-stage general sales tax, to apply at a stage prior to the retail stage and if necessary, to be combined with a separate tax on retail sales. Sub-group C considered the possibilities of a common single-stage tax at the production stage, with a separate tax at the retail stage if required. *Cf.* A. Easson, *Tax Law and Policy in the EEC*, London 1980, p. 76.
7. 'The EEC Reports on Tax Harmonization', An Unofficial Translation prepared by Dr. M. Thurston, *International Bureau of Fiscal Documentation* 1963, pp. 1–93.
8. *Idem*, pp. 94–157.
9. *Idem* at p. 73 and p. 154.
10. Professor Shoup of the United States was also a member.

the turnover tax burden on the specific commodity and consequently . . . when the principle of country of destination is applied . . . the amount of the corresponding countervailing duties or funds'.[11]

The recommendation to adopt the value added tax can be viewed as a rather audacious one, since the tax existed in only one of the Member States, namely in France. The Neumark-report did not consider the retail sales tax as a suitable alternative,[12] on the practical grounds of fiscal technicalities, particularly those relating to the large number of small retailer merchants, most of whom were thought unable to keep adequate books.[13]

The EEC-Commission agreed with the findings of the ABC-and Neumark-reports and proposed, in a draft-Directive, that harmonization should proceed in three stages. During the first stage – within four years of the Directive – Member States would abandon their multi-stage cumulative turnover taxes and replace it by a non-cumulative system of their choice. During the second stage, to be ended on 31 December 1969, the end of the transition-period, the non-cumulative systems should be replaced by a common value added tax system. The last stage, for which no time-limit was mentioned, should lead to the abolition of intra-Community tax-frontiers.

The proposal was transmitted to the European Parliament. The Internal Market Committee of the Parliament advised reduction of the envisaged three stages to two.[14] There seemed little point in changing to non-cumulative systems, in some states possibly a single-stage system, as a temporary measure, if the VAT would be introduced eventually in all states.[15] This objection was accepted by the Commission, and resulted in the submittal of two (revised) draft-Directives to the Council of Ministers.

---

11. Neumark-report, p. 139.
12. *Idem*, p. 140.
13. In fact, the Neumark-report considered the problem of applying the VAT in the retail stage so intractable that it recommended the exclusion of the retail stage from the value added tax. p. 142.
14. In a report, named after the chairman of the Committee, M. Arved Deringer, 'the Deringer-Report'.
15. Of special interest (*Cf.* Easson, note 6 *supra*, p. 78) is the interpretation of article 99 in the Deringer-report, viewed as not only requiring that the turnover taxes, excise duties and other indirect taxes be harmonized, but that they be harmonized *in their relationship* to each other. Since no attempt had been made to do this it was prophetically observed: 'On this basis, it will be necessary in twenty years time to open one's case between Emmerich and Arnhem, Wasserbillig and Trier, between Erquelines and Jeumont, between Strasbourg and Kehl, Ventimiglia and Menton, to prove to customs that one has not wrapped cigars inside one's pyjamas.' Deringer-report, Parliament Europeen: Document de Seance 1963–64, No. 56, p. 33. In view of the Commission's White Paper (See *infra*, chapter XI) the report's prophecy is even valid for thirty years.

VIII.3 FIRST AND SECOND DIRECTIVES[16]

The basic philosophy of the EEC is apparent from the preamble of the *First Directive*: . . . the main objective of the Treaty is to establish, within the framework of an economic union, a common market within which there is healthy competition and whose characteristics are similar to those of a domestic market. The attainment of this objective, the preamble continues, presupposes the prior application in Member States of legislation concerning turnover taxes such as will not distort conditions of competition or hinder the free movement of goods and services within the common market. The preamble continues that in light of the studies made, it has become clear that such harmonization must result in the abolition of cumulative multi-stage taxes and the adoption by all Member States of a common system of value added tax. Such a system of value added tax achieves the highest degree of simplicity and of neutrality when the tax is levied in as general a manner as possible and when its scope covers all stages of production and distribution and the provision of services. Therefore, – thus states the preamble – it is in the interest of the common market and of Member States to adopt a common system which shall also apply to the retail trade. However the application of that tax to retail trade might in some Member States meet with practical and political difficulties. Therefore Member States are permitted to apply the common system only up to and including the wholesale trade stage and to apply as appropriate, a separate complementary tax, at the retail level. Even if the rates and exemptions are not harmonized this should result in neutrality in competition in that within each country similar goods will bear the same tax burden, whatever the length of the production or distribution chain, and since in international trade the amount of tax burden borne by goods is known so that an exact equalization of that amount may be ensured.

Based on the above reproduced considerations from the preamble, the Member States were free, during the first stage, which the First (and Second) Directive intended to cover, to decide upon the applicable rates and, to a large extent, the exemptions.[17] The First Directive instructed the Member States to replace their present turnover taxes, not later than 1 January 1970,[18] by the common system of value added tax, which is based on the principle that a *general tax on consumption*[19] is applied to goods and services, which is exactly proportional to the price, whatever the number of transactions which

16. Dir. 67/227/EEC and Dir. 67/228/EEC, 11 April 1967, J.O. 71.
17. Article 10, par. 2. Second Directive.
18. Article 1, First Directive, however, the Third, Fourth and Fifth Directive extended this deadline.
19. The wording of the Directive indicates the legal character (*cf.* Chapter II *supra*); the indirect character follows from article 99 of the EEC-Treaty, *see* note 5 *supra*.

take place in the production and distribution process before the stage at which tax is charged.[20]

The common system of value added tax was set out in the *Second Directive*, which provided that the value added tax should apply to:

a. the supply of goods and the provision of services within the territory of the country by a taxable person against payment;

b. the importation of goods.[21]

The expressions 'territory of the country', 'taxable person', 'supply of goods', 'provision of services' were further defined.[22] The tax should be calculated on the basis of the consideration or price for the supply of goods or provision of the service or, in the case of importation, on the customs value of the goods.[23] Member States were free to establish their own standard rate of tax and to subject certain goods and services to increased or reduced rates.[24] However according to the preamble[25] the application of zero-rates should be strictly limited. Moreover imported goods should be taxed at the same rate as that applied internally to the supply of goods.[26] Also, subject to consultation, the Member States were free to determine their own exemptions.[27]

A taxable person was required to keep sufficiently detailed accounts and to issue an invoice in respect of goods supplied and services provided by him to another taxable person.[28] He was authorized to deduct[29] from the tax for which he is liable the value added tax invoiced to him in respect of his purchases and imports, where these goods and services were used for the purposes of his undertakings.[30]

Within this framework Member States were free to adopt special measures to simplify the procedures or prevent fraud[31] or to apply a special system to small undertakings whose subjection to the normal system of VAT would meet with difficulties,[32] or to apply a special system, best suited to national requirements and possibilities, to the agricultural sector, until further proposals for Directives or common procedures had been accepted.[33]

---

20. Article 2, First Directive.
21. Article 2, Second Directive.
22. Articles 3, 4, 5, 6, 7, Second Directive.
23. Article 8, Second Directive.
24. Article 9, Second Directive.
25. Fifth consideration, preamble Second Directive.
26. Article 9, par. 3, Second Directive.
27. Article 10, par. 2, Second Directive.
28. Article 12, Second Directive.
29. Article 11, Second Directive.
30. However, Member States were allowed to apply in respect of capital goods the method of deduction by annual installments, the so-called deductions *pro-rata temporis*, article 17, Second Directive; *cf.* the income-type of value added tax, under Chapter V *supra*.
31. Article 13, Second Directive.
32. Article 14, Second Directive.
33. Article 15, Second Directive.

The two directives were adopted unanimously by the Council of Ministers. At this point it is interesting to note how, in 1967, few articles were deemed to be necessary to harmonize a tax, that was considered crucial in the functioning of the customs union. Considering the sometimes very extensive Directives which followed, the thought of a 'Community VAT-code' (in the form of a regulation) cannot always be suppressed.

VIII.4 THIRD, FOURTH AND FIFTH DIRECTIVES[34]

Adoption of the necessary national legislation to implement the First and Second Directives did not cause serious difficulties in most Member States.[35] In France, the long pre-existing system of 'taxe sur la valeur ajoutée' had to be adapted on a number of (after all essential) points. Germany too was prompt in implementing the obligations set forth in the Directives, the new system entered in force there in 1968. The tax was introduced in the Netherlands at the beginning of 1969, and in Luxembourg one year later. Major difficulties were encountered in Belgium and Italy. In Belgium the main problem[36] was the fear that introduction of the new tax would have serious budgetary repercussions. Since most of the revenue from the existing turnover tax was collected by means of prepaid stamps, the change to the new system would cause a gap in the flow of revenue.

In Italy introduction of the new tax met with serious difficulties mainly[37] because the value added tax was proposed as part of a general plan of (necessary) tax reforms. This coupling of the VAT with other issues influenced the discussions about introduction of the VAT.[38]

A Third Directive extended the deadline for implementation of the First and Second Directive until 1972. The Belgian value added tax came into force in 1971. Two further directives were necessary, extending the time limit for Italy, before value added tax was eventually introduced in 1973, the year, incidentally, in which the newly acceded Member States also completed their obligations to introduce the value added tax.[39]

---

34. Dir. 69/643/EEC, 9 December 1969, J.O. L320; Dir. 71/401/EEC, 20 December 1971, J.O. L283; Dir. 72/259/EEC, 4 July 1972, J.O. L162.
35. *See generally* Donald J. Puchala, *Fiscal Harmonization in the European Communities, National Politics and International Cooperation*. London and Dover 1984.
36. *See further* Easson, *op. cit.* note 6 *supra*, p. 82, and Puchala. *See* previous note.
37. *Idem.*
38. *See further* A. Pedone, 'Italy', p. 208 in M. Aaron (ed), *VAT Experiences of Some European Countries*, Deventer 1982.
39. Denmark had already introduced the VAT in 1967 (*cf.* Chapter IV Section 2.3 *supra*), notably before accession to the EC and even before the Directives themselves were accepted. Ireland likewise introduced the VAT before accession in 1972. The UK adopted

VIII.5 BACKGROUND OF THE SIXTH DIRECTIVE

The implementation of the First and Second Directives was the first stage in the harmonization of the turnover taxes in the Community. The common system, however, based on these directives permitted the Member States such a discretion that, in 1973, really nine different and separate systems of national laws existed rather than one common Community system.[40] Major areas that were applied differently in the various Member States were agriculture, the retail stage, exemptions, deduction of tax on imports and the treatment of services across frontiers, the latter perhaps creating the most serious of problems. The national rules as to where and when services were deemed performed, whether a supply was deemed one of goods or a provision of services, and whether a transaction was deemed an exportation, varied considerably. This resulted in double taxation or the absence of taxation, distorting intra-Community commerce.[41] The Sixth Directive[42] aims at a further harmonization of the various national laws.[43] From the preamble one could derive that the second stage (as envisaged by the First and Second Directives) is the purpose of the Sixth Directive, namely the abolishment of the imposition of tax on the importation and the abolishment of remission of tax on exportation in the intra-Community commerce.

The Sixth Directive does not (intend to) accomplish this at all. The so-called border tax adjustments remain necessary. (We will return to this subject in the following chapters.) The main reason for the Sixth Directive can be found in the so-called 'own resources decision'. The previously mentioned problem areas under the First and Second Directive are extensively covered by the Sixth Directive; they will be dealt with under Section VIII.6.

---

the VAT in the same year as Italy.

Regarding the Member States that acceeded afterwards, Spain introduced the VAT in 1986. Portugal followed in 1988. The Hellenic Republic however needed a directive (the Fifteenth) to extend the time limit, agreed upon at the accession, till 1987.

40. *See* P. Derouin, *La Taxe Sur la Valeur Ajoutée dans la CEE*, 1977, in the conclusions to part one, cited by Easson, *op. cit.*, note 6, p. 84.
41. *See* more extensive on these differences, Easson, *op. cit.*, note 6, pp. 84–87.
42. Dir. 77/388/EEC, 17 May 1977, O.J. L145.
43. One may wonder whether a further harmonization was necessary, at least to the extent the Sixth Directive offers. Except for the treatment of services across borders, the other differences alluded to, do not seem to be crucial for the establishment of a common market. The necessity for detailed harmonization if not uniform legislation becomes much more predominant when a community tax is introduced, next to harmonized national taxes. *See* VIII.5.1 *infra.*

VIII.5.1 Own Resources Decision

The most pressing reason for further harmonization was the Council of Ministers' Decision of 21 April 1970, regarding the replacement of financial contributions from the Member States by the Community's own resources.[44] This 'own resources decision' provided that as from the beginning of 1975 the budget of the Community should include, in addition to customs duties and agricultural levies, revenue accruing from the value added tax by applying a rate not exceeding 1 per cent[45] to an assessment basis which is determined in a uniform manner for Member States according to Community rules.

Thus the '1 per cent' mentioned in article 4 of the Council's Decision is not meant to be 1 per cent of the total tax yield, but of the basis of assessment. Basically this 1 per cent can be considered as an additional levy, a *European tax*, on behalf of the Community in addition to the rates by the national states on their own behalf, albeit the European rate is concealed in the national rates. It should be clear that differences in national rates do not affect the proportional share in the European levy. The only provision that is necessary is a uniform as possible scope to the value added tax. The Member States will bear a fair share of the 'tax burden', based on their own resources decision, only if the basis of assessment (for private consumption) is identical in all Member States. If for example Germany taxes all consumptive expenditures and the Netherlands taxes one half of the supplies of goods and services, it is clear that Germany will 'contribute' in proportion twice as much. Thus, elimination of a number of differences stemming from the First and Second Directives were required in order to secure an equitable distribution of the fiscal burden between the Member States as well as between the, now European, taxpayers.

VIII.6 SIXTH DIRECTIVE

VIII.6.1 Introduction

The new rules introduced by the Sixth Directive cover most of the areas that need more precise definition to achieve closer harmonization of national VAT laws: territorial application, taxable transactions, place of taxable transactions, chargeable events and chargeability of tax, rates and exemptions, deductions, persons liable for payment of tax and their obligations. Special schemes are offered for small undertakings, farmers, travel-agents, and second-hand goods. The Directive also provides for an Advisory Com-

---

44. Dec. 70/243 O.J. 1970, L94/19.
45. Increased to 1.4 per cent by the Fontainebleau Agreement of 1984.

mittee on VAT, to be set up at Community level, to examine questions concerning the application of the Directive. We shall confine ourselves here to the main points of the Directive. Under Section VIII.6.11 a birds-eye view of the Sixth Directive is presented.

VIII.6.2 Territorial Application

The tax applies to the supply of goods or services effected for consideration *within the territory* of the country by a taxable person acting as such and to the importation of goods (article 2). This territorial application is further elaborated in article 3, mainly by referring to the territorial application of the EEC-Treaty.[46] As will be seen this territorial application does not exclude the embracement of a universal concept regarding the taxability of persons nor an extension of the territorial application beyond the limited scope, provided the zero-rate is used (*see* Chapter IX).

VIII.6.3 Taxable Transactions

Supply of goods is stated to mean the transfer of the right to dispose of tangible property as owner (article 5, par. 1). Tangible property includes electricity current, gas, heat, refrigeration and the like (article 5, par. 2). Also included are transfers made in connection with a compulsory purchase, or pursuant to a contract for hire purchase or conditional sale (article 5, par. 3). The private use by a taxable person, or other appropriation for nonbusiness purposes is also treated as a supply made for consideration (article 5, par. 6). States may consider as taxable supplies the transfer of immovable property and certain other transactions (article 5, par. 5). The fact that the taxability of these transactions is optional, reflects in my view a misperception of consumption. Only if consumption in its literal sense is regarded as the basis of taxation and not expenditure (*see* Chapter II.3 *supra*), land itself, being a commodity which is not consumed, does not seem appropriate for inclusion in the tax.[47] The Sixth Directive leaves this particular problem unresolved. Another optional taxable supply is the application of self-constructed goods, where the VAT on such goods, had they been acquired from another taxable person, would not be wholly deductible (article 5, par. 7). This may be

---

46. Article 227. *See* however, The Eleventh Directive under Section VIII.7 *infra*. From the scope of the VAT (article 2 of the Sixth Directive) it follows that the principle of the country of destination is applied (*cf.* Chapter III *supra*). We will return to this principle under Chapters IX and X *infra*.
47. *Cf.* Easson, *op. cit.* note 6 *supra,* p. 86 and his note 84.

necessary to avoid the elimination of regular supplying patterns. When the tax is not fully deductible self-construction results in a lower tax burden, than on a purchase of a ready-made good, since the wage (and profit) components remain untaxed (*see also* Chapter VI.4.4 *supra*).

Supply of Services is defined on a residual basis to mean any transaction which does not constitute a supply of goods; it includes assignments of intangible property (article 6, par. 1).

Self-supply or the use for other nonbusiness purposes is also treated as a taxable service (article 6, par. 2). States may derogate from this provided it does not lead to distortion of competition.

Importation of goods is stated to mean the entry of goods in the territory of the country (article 7).

VIII.6.4 Taxable Persons

Taxable person means any person who *independently* carries out in any place any economic activity – specified to comprise all activities of producers, traders and persons supplying services, including mining and agricultural activities, and activities of the professions – whatever the purpose or results of that activity (article 4, par. 1 and 2). Thus, consistent with the nature of the value added tax, it is irrelevant whether or not the supply is made for profit, it is the expenditure that counts. The requirement that a taxable person acts in an 'independent' capacity excludes employees from an obligation to charge value added tax on services provided to their employers. It is at the discretion of Member States to tax occasional transactions (article 4, par. 3) as well as to treat associated enterprises as a single, taxable entity, although they are legally independent, provided they are closely bound to one another by financial, economic and organizational links (article 4, par. 4). Governmental entities are not normally considered to be taxable persons in respect of activities engaged in that capacity, except if they compete with commercial enterprises, such as in telecommunications, the transport of goods and passengers, and the supply of water, gas, and electricity (article 4, par. 5 and Annex D).

Although the delivery of goods or the performance of services triggers a taxable event, the Directive also provides that a taxable event may arise, or at least tax liability occurs, when a supplier issues an invoice for goods or services (article 10, par. 2). In general, the *liability* to pay VAT rests on the taxable person who carries out taxable transactions. When the taxable person resides abroad, Member States may adopt arrangements whereby the tax is payable by some one other than the taxable person residing abroad or the latter may be held jointly or severally liable for payment of the tax (article 21, par. 1). See further on this so-called 'deferred payment' under Chapter XI *infra*.

Also the *obligations* of persons liable for payments are summed up in detail including the obligation to submit returns jointly with payment of the net amount, the obligation to maintain records of the sales and purchases, as well as of the tax charged on those transactions, the obligation to issue invoices, etc.

From the definition of importation of goods, in which taxable persons are not defined as such, it follows that *everyone* is a taxable person regarding the importation of goods. Thus the indirect character of the tax is subject to one general exception namely when the consumer imports goods him- or herself.

The person *liable* to pay the VAT on importation is the person (or are the persons) designated or accepted as such by the Member States into which the goods are imported (article 21, par. 2).

VIII.6.5 Place of Taxable Transactions

From the territorial application and the definitions of taxable persons and taxable transactions various conclusions may be drawn regarding the scope of the VAT:

  a. It does not matter who is the taxable person, where he lives or where he has fixed his establishment, as long as he independently carries out economic activities, thus a universal concept is applied.
  b. These activities however are irrelevant if they consist of supplies of goods or services without a consideration, except for self-supplies.
  c. In order to be taxable the economic activities have to be performed within the territory of the (taxing) country.

Thus *non-taxable* transactions are supplies of goods or services performed by non-taxable persons, or performed without a consideration, or performed outside the territory of the country.

The question whether an activity is performed within (or outside) a territory does not necessarily receive a single answer. We shall confine ourselves here to the principal rules laid down in the Directive. We will return to the place of taxation in relation to the allocation of taxes (and the avoidance of double taxation or the absence of taxation) under chapter IX.

The general rule in the Sixth Directive is obvious. *Goods* that are not dispatched or transported, are treated as being supplied at the place where the goods are when the supply takes place (article 8, par. 1.b). The question of allocation will only occur when goods are transported or dispatched, by the seller or purchaser, in that case the place of supply is deemed to be where the transportation commences (article 8, par. 1.a).[48] For *services* in general the

---

48. But if installed by or on behalf of the suppliers, the goods are treated as supplied where installed (article 8, par. 1.a). *See also* chapter IX, note 48.

place of supply is deemed to be the place *where the supplier* has established his business or has fixed an establishment from which the service is supplied (article 9, par. 1). To this general principle, there are a large number of exceptions in order to eliminate anomalies when services are supplied in an international context. It should be noted here that in Europe the 'importation' of services is not a taxable transaction (we will return to this phenomenon under Chapter IX.4), resulting in an elaborated scheme of allocation of the place of providing services. Thus services supplied in connection with immovable property, including the services of real estate agents, contractors, architects, are deemed performed *where the property is situated* (article 9, par. 2.a). Other services such as cultural, artistic, sporting, scientific, educational or entertainment activities, or work performed on tangible movable property are deemed performed where they are *physically carried out* (article 9, par. 2.c). Likewise as are transport services, having regard to the distances covered (article 9, par. 2.b).[49] Yet a *further category* of services, when performed for customers in another country (only if he is a taxable person, if the customer is in another Member State), are taxable in the country where the customer is established. These include advertising services and services such as transfers and assignments of copyrights, patents, trademarks and similar rights, the services of consultants, engineers, lawyers, accountants, data processing services, banking, financial and insurance transactions (article 9, par. 2.e). Regarding this last category of services Member States may consider the place of supply in or outside the Community in contrast with the theretofore presented rules in order to avoid double-, or nontaxation (article 9, par. 3).

VIII.6.6 Taxable Amount and Tax Rates

Rates of tax are expressed as a percentage of the *taxable amount*, defined as everything which constitutes the consideration, which has been or is to be obtained by the supplier from the purchaser, the customer or a third party. Separate provisions are made for self-supply and other use for nonbusiness purposes (article 1.A, par. 1). The taxable amount in respect of imported goods is further elaborated for those cases where no price is paid or where the price paid or to be paid is not the sole consideration for the imported goods (article 11.B). Under Chapter II.3 *supra* the special position of second hand goods under sales taxes was mentioned. The consequence that an expenditure may occur more than once regarding the same product, has led to measures mitigating the effect of this consequence. The Directive (in article 32) allows

---

49. The rules relating to the place of supply of the hiring of movable tangible property caused too many distortions, hence the Tenth Directive was issued, *see* Section VIII.7 *infra*.

Member States to retain systems generally allowing a lower taxable amount applicable to used goods, works of art, antiques and collection items, until the Council has adopted, upon a proposal from the Commission,[50] a Community taxation system to be applied to these goods.

The *rates* are fixed by the Member States, provided the standard rate is the same for the supply of goods or services or the importation of like goods (article 12, par. 3 and 5), in conformity with the requirements of internal and external neutrality (*see* Chapter III *supra*). Member States are permitted to apply increased or reduced rates to certain categories of supplies, provided that each reduced rate is fixed at such a level as in the normal way to permit the deduction of the whole of the tax imposed upon inputs (article 12, par. 4). The reason for this requirement is apparently derived from the objections to the granting of tax refunds, hence the so-called 'butoir' or 'buffer-rule' (*see* Section VI. 4.2 *supra*). From a theoretical point of view this requirement can hardly be justified, since the burden of the tax falls ultimately upon the consumer.[51] Whether a taxable person accounts for tax collected or receives a refund in respect of under-collection is irrelevant, since he is merely an unpaid tax official who collects the money.[52]

VIII.6.6.1 Zero-Rates

From the requirement that reduced rates should normally permit the deduction of input taxes, it follows that the Sixth Directive regards zero-rates as incompatible, in principle, with the VAT-system. A somewhat confusing aspect in this objection is that the Directive itself prescribes a whole range of zero-rated transactions, albeit under the name of exemptions. Basically, these exemptions, with the right to a deduction or a refund of the value added tax (*see* article 17, par. 3), are related to international transactions. Their intention is to safeguard the principle of the country of destination, which requires that exports are exempted; the nature of these exemptions is of a purely technical character. In addition to these prescribed zero-rates, the Sixth Directive permits Member States to retain those zero-rates that were in force at the end of 1975 (article 28, par. 2), if applied for a clearly defined social reason and for the benefit of the final consumer (as permitted under the Second Directive, article 17 last indent) until a date fixed by the Council, or until such time as the tax frontiers are abolished. As mentioned before from a theoretical point of view the objections against reduced rates, which include

50. Since 1978 a proposal (Seventh Directive) awaited adoption by the Council, recently it has been withdrawn (*see* Section VIII.7 *infra*).
51. Easson, *op. cit.* note 6, *supra*, p. 92.
52. J. Reugebrink, 'The Sixth Directive for the Harmonization of Value Added Tax', C.M.L. Rev. 1978, p. 313.

zero-rates, cannot be justified. However, in light of the own-resources decision zero-rates (and extremely reduced rates) may cause a problem. Although the transactions remain within the tax system and tax returns are still made thereon, so that a Member State can make its calculations of the amount of tax due to the Community, the application of zero-rates will result in subsidizing those transactions to the extent of the tax (rate) imposed by the Community on them. The same is valid for rates reduced to a level below the Community tax rate. It should be added that this subsidy infringes upon one of the aims of the Community, the realization of a system ensuring that competition is not at all distorted. In any case, difficulties regarding the own resources will arise, if zero-rating is applied as an alternative to exemptions – how attractive this may be from the perspective of a most efficient VAT – since exemptions do not form part of the tax base for the own resources. This explains well the detailed enumeration of the exemptions in the Sixth Directive.

VIII.6.7 Exemptions

From the foregoing it follows that it was necessary to standardize exemptions in order to achieve a common base of assessment for the own resources. There are two lists of exemptions, one concerning activities exempted in the public interest and one concerning other exempted activities. The former includes matters such as postal, medical, social, educational and cultural services (article 13.A). As for the other exemptions, these include under certain conditions, insurance and re-insurance transactions, the leasing or letting of immovable property, the letting of premises or sites for parking vehicles or the hire of safes, banking and financial transactions with certain exceptions (article 13.B).

Taxable persons are not allowed a right of option for taxation except in specified transactions relating to immovable property (article 13.C). During a transitional period Member States are allowed to continue to tax some activities which are exempt under the Directive (Annex E), to continue to exempt some taxable activities (Annex F) or to grant taxable persons the option to choose for taxation or exemption (Annex G) under certain conditions (article 28). Furthermore the Directive provides for various exemptions (with the right to a deduction) of exports and like transactions and international transport, mainly to safeguard the principle of the country of destination (articles 15, 16). The exemptions on importation will be dealt with under VIII.6.10.

VIII.6.8 Deductions

The essence of the VAT is the deduction of input tax in the non-consumer sphere. Under the Sixth Directive a taxable person has the right to deduct from the tax for which he is accountable in respect of his supplies, the tax invoiced to him on goods or services supplied to, or imported by him. This right arises at the moment when the deductible tax becomes chargeable (article 17, par. 1), in other words as soon as the invoice has been issued. In case of a right to a refund, Member States may carry the excess forward to the following tax period (article 18). The right to a deduction or refund of the VAT is restricted in so far as the goods and services are used for the purposes of his taxable transactions (article 17, par. 2) including taxable transactions in another country provided that the transactions would be eligible for deduction of tax if they had occurred in the territory of the (home) country (article 17, par. 3).

Thus no deduction is permitted for goods and services supplied in respect of exempt transactions or non-business purposes. A trader who uses goods and services both for taxed transactions and for other purposes - exempt or nonbusiness - may consequently deduct only the (proportion of the) tax that is attributable to the former transactions (article 17, par. 5). The Directive provides for calculation methods of the deductible proportion (article 19). Furthermore the Directive provides various rules governing the exercise of the right to deduct such as the possession of an invoice, drawn up in accordance with the rules thereof, or of an import document (article 18).

VIII.6.8.1 Deductions and Investment Goods

The basic principle of a consumption type value added tax is retained in the Sixth Directive. A taxable person has a right to deduct (immediately and fully) the tax on investment or capital goods. Deductions, however, in the case of investment goods may lead, if no rule were made to cover a charge occurring in the deductible proportion during the lifetime of the good, to an unjustified advantage or disadvantage for the taxable person. Provisions therefore are made for a limited period during which the original deduction can be adjusted if it turns out to be excessive or inadequate. The Directive provides for a five-year adjustment period, deemed to correspond to the normal depreciation period. In each year one fifth of the tax paid on the investment good when it was purchased is to be adjusted in proportion to the actual use (article 20, par. 2). Member States retain discretion to extend this period up to ten years.

Further it is provided that in case of supply during the period of adjustment, capital goods shall be regarded as if they had still been applied totally for business use by the taxable person until expiration of the adjustment period. Such business activities are presumed fully taxable in cases where the delivery of these goods is taxed; they are presumed fully exempt, where the delivery is exempt (article 20, par.3). Thus in the former case full deduction is allowed for the remaining time of the adjustment period and in the latter no deduction whatsoever, often resulting in the obligation to reimburse the (partially) deducted tax.

VIII.6.9 Special Schemes

The Sixth Directive offers various special schemes for small undertakings, farmers, travel agents, (article 24, 25, 26). Member States applying a special system to used goods, works of art, antiques and collectors' items may retain that system until a Community taxation system to be applied to these goods has been adopted (article 32). Only the special scheme for small undertakings and the so-called common flat-rate scheme for farmers will be dealt with here.

VIII.6.9.1 Small Undertakings

The Directive requires a taxable person to maintain records of his sales and purchases as well as of the tax charged on those transactions (article 22). To keep a record of that type may be beyond the capabilities of certain retailers and other small taxpayers since they do not usually issue invoices to their customers or make any written or printed record at the time when a sale takes place. This special scheme for small undertakings (article 24) allows, provisionally, Member States to use simplified procedures such as flat-rate schemes for changing and collecting the tax but requires that there be no tax reduction involved. The intention of this provision is apparently to reduce the administrative burden on small enterprises and not the taxes, as is the intention of reduced rates or exemptions. Member States are permitted to exempt taxable persons with an annual turnover not exceeding 5000 European units of accounts; this sales related exemption clearly results in both administrative simplification and a tax reduction.

Since annual turnover is not necessarily the best indicator of size or ability to bear the burden, the scheme for small business is unsatisfactory in a number of respects, especially the neutrality in tax base and budgeting problems caused thereby. The Directive announces the intended introduction of a common special scheme to be decided upon by the Council at the appropriate time.[53]

---

53. *See* the proposal of 9 October 1986, O.J. 1986, C 272.

VIII.6.9.2 Farmers

A special scheme is also offered for the agricultural sector by the Sixth Directive. This is because farmers are considered another group that may lack the detailed records necessary for a VAT-return. Unlike the vast majority of small businesses, the administrative problems of farmers cannot be solved by establishing an exemption up to a certain sales level. In contrast with most small businesses, that sell to final consumers, farmers sell primarily to manufacturers, wholesalers and other taxable persons. An exemption will consequently lead to accumulation of taxes (*cf.* Chapter VI.4.4 *supra*). In order to avoid this and to ensure tax neutrality the Directive offers a special scheme, known as the common flat-rate scheme, in which the following mechanism is applied: the supplies by the farmer under the special scheme are exempt but the farmer qualifies for flat rate compensation to offset the value added tax charged to him on inputs. The compensation, which the customers/entrepreneurs are allowed to deduct – in effect the deduction which would otherwise be available to farmers is passed forward to their customers – is calculated as a percentage fixed by the Member State and applied to the farmers turnover. Since the states themselves calculate the charge on inputs, it must be feared that the desired neutrality in the tax base is impaired and budgetary difficulties are caused.[54]

VIII.6.10 Importation of Goods

Most of the subjects dealt with heretofore are either also applicable to the imports, or the importation of goods has been separately mentioned. Two aspects need further attention, the exemptions and the obligations of persons liable for payment in respect of imports.

VIII.6.10.1 Exemptions

The exemptions on importation encompass those which are applicable (in all circumstances) regarding the supplies by taxable persons *within* the country. Hence, the external neutrality is guaranteed (article 14, par. 1.a). Furthermore various exemptions are enumerated, which either have their source in customs formalities, like transit, temporary importation arrangements and the like or in the exemptions from customs duties as provided for in the CCT or in international agreements (articles 14, par. 1.b till g, and 16, par. 1.A). Also, the supply of services, in connection with the importation of goods is included in the taxable amount (article 14, par. 1.i). Further clarification of

---

54. Easson, *op. cit.* note 6 *supra*, p. 95.

the scope of the exemptions and detailed rules for their implementation have prescribed by the Directive.

VIII.6.10.2 Obligations in Respect of Imports

It is left to the Member States to lay down the rules for the making of the declarations and payments. These rules are generally copied from the rules regarding customs declarations. However, Member States may provide that the value added tax payable on importation of goods by taxable persons or persons liable to tax need not be paid at the time of importation on condition that the tax is mentioned as such in the return, which is regularly submitted regarding the supplies (article 23). We will return to this so-called post-poned accounting system under Chapter XI.

*VIII.6.11 Bird's Eye View of the Sixth Directive**

* PREAMBLE

* INTRODUCTORY PROVISIONS

– modifications of VAT according to the following (art.1.):

* SCOPE (art. 2.)

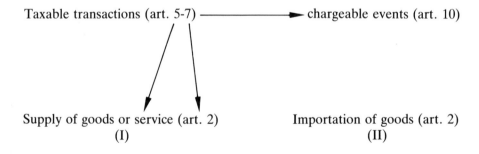

Taxable transactions (art. 5-7) ⟶ chargeable events (art. 10)

Supply of goods or service (art. 2)　　　　Importation of goods (art. 2)
(I)　　　　　　　　　　　　　　(II)

* i.e. taxed at zero-rate.

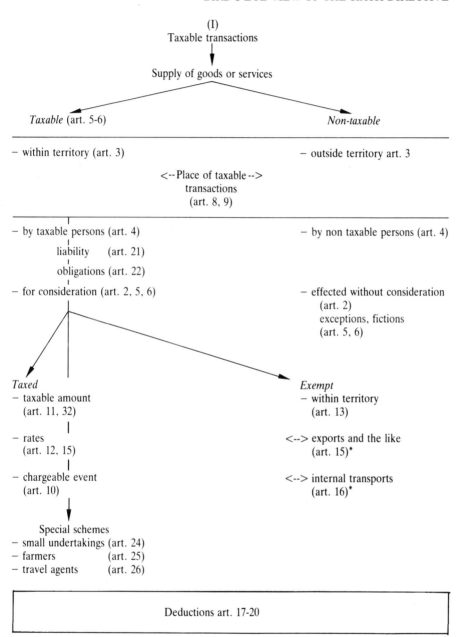

(I)
Taxable transactions

Supply of goods or services

Taxable (art. 5-6)   *Non-taxable*

– within territory (art. 3)   – outside territory art. 3

                        < -- Place of taxable -->
                            transactions
                            (art. 8, 9)

– by taxable persons (art. 4)   – by non taxable persons (art. 4)
        liability   (art. 21)
        obligations (art. 22)
– for consideration (art. 2, 5, 6)   – effected without consideration
                                                    (art. 2)
                                                    exceptions, fictions
                                                    (art. 5, 6)

Taxed   *Exempt*
– taxable amount   – within territory
   (art. 11, 32)   (art. 13)

– rates   <--> exports and the like
   (art. 12, 15)   (art. 15)*

– chargeable event   <--> internal transports
   (art. 10)   (art. 16)*

        Special schemes
– small undertakings (art. 24)
– farmers   (art. 25)
– travel agents   (art. 26)

Deductions art. 17-20

* i.e. taxed at zero-rate.

(II)

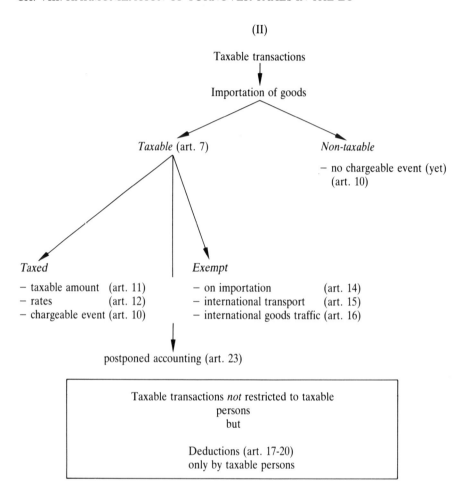

Taxable transactions

Importation of goods

Taxable (art. 7)   Non-taxable

                                           − no chargeable event (yet)
                                             (art. 10)

Taxed

− taxable amount (art. 11)
− rates   (art. 12)
− chargeable event (art. 10)

Exempt

− on importation   (art. 14)
− international transport   (art. 15)
− international goods traffic (art. 16)

postponed accounting (art. 23)

Taxable transactions *not* restricted to taxable
persons
but

Deductions (art. 17-20)
only by taxable persons

− Simplification procedures   (art. 27.)
− Transitional provision   (art. 28.)
− Value added tax committee (art. 29.)
− Miscellaneous   (art. 30-33.)
− Final provisions   (art. 34-38.)

VIII.7 Other Directives and Proposals for Directives

ˑSince the adoption of the Sixth Directive fourteen (numbered) directives have been submitted to the Council of Ministers. A detailed analysis of these directives falls beyond the scope of this book. I restrict myself to the following summary.

Eight of the proposed directives have been adopted by the Council,[55] The ninth Council Directive and the fifteenth extended the time-limit for several Member States to implement the Sixth Directive.[56]

The Eight and Thirteenth Directives deal with the refund of VAT to taxable persons not established in the territory of the Member State *c.q.* to persons not established in Community territory.

The Tenth Directive deals with the rules relating to the place of supply of the hiring of movable tangible property,[57] whereas the Eleventh Directive excludes the French overseas departments from the scope of the Sixth Directive.[58] The Seventeenth Directive covers the exemption from VAT on the temporary importation of goods (other than means of transport). The Twentieth Directive authorizes Germany to compensate farmers for the dismantlement of monetary compensatory amounts, using VAT as an instrument.

Three of the six proposals, not yet adopted, have been withdrawn recently, namely the Seventh draft Directive, dealing with a common system of VAT to be applied to works of art, collectors items, antiques and used goods,[59] the proposal for a Fourteenth Directive, proposing the compulsary application of deferred payment (post-poned accounting) of the tax payable on importation by taxable persons,[60] and the proposal for a Sixteenth Directive dealing with the importation of goods by private persons.[61]

For the Seventh draft Directive new proposals are announced. The deferred payment and the proposals regarding the importation by private persons have been replaced by the far-reaching proposals as follow-up to the white Paper (see chapter XII *infra*).

Regarding the remaining proposals[62] dealing with expenditures not eligible

---

55. Eight, 79/1072/EEC, O.J. L331; Ninth, 78/583/EEC, O.J. L194; Tenth, 84/386/EEC, O.J. L208; Eleventh, 80/368/EEC, O.J. L90; Thirteenth, 86/560/EEC, O.J. L326; Fifteenth, 83/648/EEC, O.J. L360; Seventeenth, 85/362/EEC, O.J. L192; Twentieth, 85/361/EEC, O.J. L192.
56. *Cf.* note 39 *supra.*
57. *Cf.* note 49 *supra.*
58. *Cf.* note 46 *supra.*
59. O.J. 1979, C 136, *cf.* note 50 *supra.*
60. O.J. 1982, C 201. *See also* Section XI.5.3. *infra.*
61. O.J. 1984, C 226. *See also* Section IX.4.1.1 *infra* regarding case 15/81 (Gaston Schul).
62. Twelfth draft, O.J. 1983, C 37; Eighteenth draft, O.J. 1984, C 347; Nineteenth draft, O.J. 1984, C 347.

for deduction of VAT (Twelfth draft Directive), the abolition of certain derogations from the Sixth Directive (Eighteenth draft Directive), and other contributions to an increased degree of uniformity in the assessement basis for collection of own resources (Nineteenth draft Directive), in the White Paper the Commission urges the Council to deal with these proposals as a matter of urgency. All these directives and proposals for directives however do not lead to the abolition of intra-Community tax frontiers; we will now turn to this subject in the following chapters.

Chapter IX. The Issue of Border Tax Adjustments

IX.1 INTRODUCTION

The issue of border tax adjustments re-emerges in discussions of world trade with a certain regularity. Border tax adjustments is a fairly new term which refers to the treatment of taxes under the rules of the General Agreement on Tariffs and Trade (GATT).[1] The provisions on the international treatment of internal taxes in the GATT are interpreted to permit border tax adjustments for indirect taxes, but not for direct taxes.

These border tax adjustments consist of a surcharge on imports, not to exceed those internal taxes or other internal charges applied to like domestic products, and a rebate on exports of duties and taxes in amounts not in excess of those which have accrued. The taxation on importation and remission on exportation are also called 'tax frontiers',[2] 'tax boundaries' or 'tax barriers'.[3]

The application of border tax adjustments is permissive, rather than mandatory.[4] The Contracting Parties to the GATT may impose compensatory taxes on imports and may exempt, or remit taxes on exports, but there is no requirement that they do so. Member States of the European Community are subject, as Contracting Parties, to the rules of the GATT in their trade with non-Member States.[5] Therefore application of border tax adjustments for the indirect taxes, including VAT, is permitted in their external trade by all the Member States.

---

1. General Agreement on Tariffs and Trade, 30 October 1947 no. 1700, 55 U.N.T.S. 187, (hereinafter cited as GATT).
2. *See* J. Reugebrink, 'The Sixth Directive for the Harmonization of Value Added Tax', C.M.L. Rev. 1978, p. 310.
3. *See* the White Paper, Chapter XI *infra*. Although a distinction can be made between 'boundary' and 'frontier' we will employ the words interchangeably as if they are synonymous. (A boundary denotes a line whereas a frontier is more properly a region or zone having width as well as length, A.O. Cukwurah, *The Settlement of Boundary Disputes in International Law*, Manchester 1967, p. 11.)
4. A.J. Easson, *Tax Law and Policy in the EEC*, London 1980, p. 61.
5. As to the legal effects of the GATT rules *See* J.H. Jackson, 'The puzzle of GATT, J.W.T.L. 1976, pp. 131–161. *See further*, M. Waelbroeck, 'Effect of GATT within the legal order of the EEC, J.W.T.L. 1976, pp. 614–623.

Articles 95 – 98 of the EEC Treaty also apply, or rather permit the application of border tax adjustments in intra-Community trade. A modification of the GATT rules has been proposed since unfavorable trade effects resulting from the adjustments are assumed. A proposal has even been made for the elimination of border tax adjustments altogether.[6] Such a decision to eliminate border tax adjustments on indirect taxes would most probably have had a large trade inhibiting effect.[7]

During the Tokyo Round,[8] the proposal to eliminate border tax adjustments was rejected. The existing practices were confirmed. As regards the intra-Community trade the European Commission has proposed on several occasions to eliminate the tax barriers caused by the Value Added Tax. We will return to these proposals in the following chapters. In this chapter we will deal with the phenomenon of border tax adjustments in general and some problems caused by it within the European Community. Specific attention will be paid to the views that until recently prevailed regarding the (removal of) tax frontiers based on the EEC-Treaty and the Sixth Directive.

IX.2 GATT

The concepts regarding subsidies and border tax adjustments are embodied in the GATT. There is no unified GATT provision dealing exclusively with border taxes. Besides Article VI, dealing with anti-dumping and countervailing duties, the GATT articles concerning border tax adjustments are Articles II (tariff concessions), III (internal taxation on imports) and Article XVI, adopted in 1955, dealing with the border tax adjustments on exports.

The Articles II and III govern border tax adjustments on *imports*. Article II prohibits import charges in excess of those provided in the GATT, but excludes from this prohibition the levy on an imported product of 'a charge equivalent to an internal tax imposed, consistently with Article III in respect of like domestic products'. Article III provides that internal taxes shall not be applied so as to afford protection to domestic production. Discrimination is also forbidden: imported products shall 'not be subject, directly or indirectly, to internal taxes or internal charges of any kind in excess of those applied, directly or indirectly, to like domestic products'.

Article XVI specifically deals with the question of border tax adjustments for *exports*.

An interpretative note was added which specifically excluded certain tax

---

6. G.M. Grossman, 'Alternative Border Tax Policies', J.W.T.L. 1978, p. 453.
7. *Idem*, p. 460.
8. The Tokyo Round is one of the major multi-lateral negotiations held under auspices of the GATT.

relief given to exporters, that is, relief for taxes *on products* from being classified subsidies,[9] declaring:

'The exemption of an exported product from duties or taxes borne by the like products when destined for domestic consumption or the remission of such duties or taxes in amounts not in excess of those which have accrued shall not be deemed to be subsidy.'

This interpretive note was itself subsequently clarified in a report by a 1960 GATT Working Party on Subsidies.[10] According to this report, tax adjustments falling within the definition of subsidies include:

'(c) The remission, calculated in relation to exports, of direct taxes . . . (d) The exemption, in respect of exported goods, of charges or taxes *other than* charges in connection with importation or *indirect* taxes levied at one or several stages on the same goods if sold for internal consumption, . . .' (emphasis added).

These were, until recently, the GATT provisions dealing with border taxes.

It has been suggested that it is a misinterpretation of the GATT provisions to assume that they were intended to neutralize (by border tax adjustments) the effect of domestic taxes on the balance of trade.[11] In fact the GATT provisions were not intended to *permit* either export rebates or import charges. Rather they were designed to *limit* these practices with regard to selective excises.[12]

Next to this suggested misinterpretation, the essence of the debate on border tax adjustments has been the conviction that the GATT rules are based on premises which may be inaccurate; that is, that the incidence of those taxes at present defined as 'indirect' is passed on in its entirety to the ultimate consumer, and that those taxes at present defined as 'direct' are borne by the corporation (or the shareholder) and are not included in any portion of the final price.[13]

Assuming these premises are inaccurate, the application of the destination principle only for indirect taxes constitutes a serious constraint on the fiscal sovereignty of those countries (such as the United States), which rely heavily

9. For a comprehensive analysis of the GATT provisions on border tax adjustments *see* R.W. Rosendahl, *'Border Tax Adjustments: Problems and Proposals' Law and Policy in International Business* 1970, p. 92 *et seq.* and J.B. Feller, 'Mutiny Against the Bounty: An Examination of Subsidies, Border Tax Adjustments', J.W.T.L. 1973, p. 490.
10. Rosendahl, *op. cit.* note 9 *supra*, p. 96.
11. R.H. Floyd, 'GATT provisions on Border Tax Adjustments', J.W.T.L. 1973, p. 490.
12. *Idem*, p. 491.
13. R.E. Latimer, 'The Border Tax Adjustment Question', *Canadian Tax Journal* 1968, p. 412.

on direct taxes to finance the public sectors.[14] The present border tax adjustments favor the use of indirect taxes or, put another way, the present border tax mechanism works to the disadvantage of those countries that rely heavily on direct taxes.[15]

Besides arguments that a disadvantage is out of the question[16] – since the introduction of an indirect tax, like VAT, leads to a rise in prices, so that a remission on exportation restores the former situation – or the argument that differences are equalized by the rates of exchange,[17] the opponents of the present border tax mechanism have suggested many solutions.

It has been proposed that the EC should harmonize border tax adjustments at some rate lower than the harmonized VAT.[18] In this proposition a grant of tax credit for taxes not paid – but which would have been paid if the border tax would have been levied at its full rate – or even the grant of an outright tax refund or subsidy on imports have been suggested. It has been admitted that this approach would be difficult to sell to the Europeans.[19]

Other proposals require unilateral action by a state relying on direct taxes.[20] For example the United States could impose countervailing duties based on (the well-known) section 303 of the Tariff Act of 1930.[21] However the *Zenith* case, decided by the Supreme Court of the United States on 21 June 1978, rejected the application of countervailing duties against indirect taxes.[22] It has been suggested that an opposite decision in the *Zenith* case leading to the imposition of countervailing duties by the United States, combined with retaliation by US trading partners, would have produced the worst of both worlds.[23]

The establishment of a more extensive system of border tax adjustments in the United States has also been suggested by expanding the indirect tax system or even by introducing a VAT.[24] The superiority of a VAT over the

---

14. M.B. Kraus, 'Border Tax Adjustments: A Potential Trans-Atlantic Trade Dispute', J.W.T.L. 1976, p. 152.
15. M Leontiades, 'The Logic of Border Taxes', *National Tax Journal* 1966, p. 173.
16. J. Reugebrink, ('Directe en indirecte belastingen een achterhaalde classificatie?' in *Cijns en Dijns*, Deventer 1975, p. 141) quotes Musgrave as the authority on the mentioned controversy.
17. P. Verloren van Thermaat, *Fiscale Harmonisatie in de EEG*, Deventer 1966, p. 11. In my view rates of exchange may have an equalizing effect, but this effect is frequently altered by the continuous shift in the balance between direct and indirect taxes. *Cf.* Reugebrink, *op. cit.* note 16 *supra*, p. 143.
18. Rosendahl, *op. cit.* note 9, p. 117.
19. *Idem*, p. 118. Clearly this proposition violates Articles 95 and 96 of the EEC Treaty.
20. *Idem*, p. 119. *See also* Feller, *op. cit.* note 9 *supra*, p. 17.
21. *See* for a comprehensive analysis Feller, *op. cit.* note 9 *supra*, pg. 19.
22. XVII I.L.M. 1978, p. 923 *et. seq.*
23. D.A. DeRosa, J.M. Finger, S.S. Golub and W.W. Nye, 'What the "Zenith Case" might have meant,' J.W.T.L. 1980, p. 54.
24. Rosendahl, *op. cit.* note 9, p. 129.

retail sales tax as presently applied in most US states will be discussed under Chapter XIII.

The most serious suggestions regarding border tax adjustments have explicitly required an international response.[25] Remedy of the inequities of the present border tax adjustments should be found in the adoption of more subtle application of the existing GATT rules.[26] For example, border tax adjustments should only be permitted to the extent that such taxes were actually shifted forward. However, the major problem is tracing this impact of a particular tax on shifting, when all other dynamic economic variables are included. This has been described as 'searching in a dark room for a black cat that isn't there'.[27]

Still the advantage of this approach to an international solution, possibly by a refinement of GATT assumptions, on the shifting of indirect taxes is the fact that the present system is accepted as basically the most workable.[28] Clearly by this approach unilateral action and consequent retaliation can be avoided. The subject of border tax adjustments needs further study and negotiation.

For the time being the present practices have been reaffirmed. Within the framework of the GATT, agreement was reached, during the Tokyo Round, on the interpretation and application of Articles VI, XVI, and XXIII of the General Agreement on Tariffs and Trade.[29] In the annex to this agreement an illustrative list of (forbidden) export subsidies is shown, including in paragraph (e)

> 'the full or partial exemption, remission or deferral, specifically related to exports, of direct taxes'.

and in paragraph (h)

> the exemption, remission or deferral of prior stage cumulative indirect taxes on goods and services used in the production of exported goods in excess of those used in the production of like products when sold for domestic consumption'.[30]

In the interpretive notes it is declared that for the purpose of this agreement paragraph (h) does not apply to value added tax systems, and border tax adjustments in lieu thereof. The problem of excessive remission of value added taxes is exclusively covered by (the following) paragraph (g). According to paragraph (g) an example of an export subsidy is

25. *Idem*, p. 129.
26. *Idem*, p. 132.
27. Leontiades, *op. cit.* note 15 *supra*, p. 178.
28. Rosendahl, *op. cit.* note 9 *supra*, p. 132.
29. XVIII I.L.M. 1979, pp. 579–620.
30. *Idem*, p. 616.

'The exemption or remission on the production and distribution of exported products, of indirect taxes in excess of those levied in respect of the production and distribution of like products when sold for domestic production'.[31]

From the foregoing it may be concluded that the present border tax adjustment system has been affirmed at an international level, preventing impending unilateral countervailing action. That does not mean that the discussion on this subject will die down or that detailed analysis on shifting tendencies and new suggestions are not to be expected in the future. However, for the time being, the Contracting Parties to the GATT may impose compensatory taxes on imports and may exempt from tax, or remit taxes on, exports, provided that these are indirect taxes. Member States of the European Community are subject, as Contracting Parties, to the rules of the GATT in their trade with non-Member States.[32] Therefore application of border tax adjustments for the indirect taxes, including VAT, is permitted in their external trade by all the Member States. The EEC-Treaty also permits the application of border tax adjustments in intra-Community trade, resulting in tax frontiers between the Member States. We will turn to this subject now.

IX.3 TAX FRONTIERS WITHIN THE EC

The objections raised against the various cumulative systems of levying sales taxes (see chapter IV *supra*) – which in Europe lead to the proposals to harmonize the different systems – can be summed up by the problem of intra-Community tax frontiers.

The existence of tax frontiers makes it fully understandable why the EEC-Treaty only mentions turnover taxes (and other forms of indirect taxes)[33] in Article 99, in asking for harmonization. These taxes lead to adjustments generally right at the borders, a situation that is pre-eminently prejudicial to the good working of the Common Market.

IX.3.1 Average Rates

Article 95 of the EEC Treaty prohibits Member States from imposing on the products of other Member States any internal taxation of any kind in excess of

31. *Idem*, p. 616.
32. *See* note 5 *supra*.
33. As will be mentioned in Chapters XI and XII, a spill-over to (harmonization of) direct taxes is inevitable. *See* for the harmonization of the indirect taxes *in their relationship* note 15, Chapter VIII.2 *supra*.

that imposed directly or indirectly on similar domestic products. When products are exported to the territory of any Member State any drawback of internal taxation shall, according to Article 96, not exceed the internal taxation imposed on them, whether directly or indirectly. In the above-mentioned articles indirect taxes are not explicitly mentioned. However, it appears by analogy with Article 99 – wherein the mandate is given to the Commission to harmonize turnover taxes, excise duties and *other forms* of *indirect taxation* – that indirect taxes are also covered by Articles 95 and 96.[34] This also follows from the application of the destination principle, which is actually prescribed in these articles.

The prohibition of fiscal discrimination embodied in the Articles 95 and 96 causes, as mentioned before, difficulties in cumulative cascade systems. In these systems the tax burden on a given product cannot be determined exactly, so that an exact settlement at the borders becomes impossible. Under Article 97 of the EEC-Treaty, Member States which levy a turnover tax calculated on a cumulative cascade tax system may, in case of internal taxation imposed by them on imported products or of drawback allowed by them on exported products, establish average rates for specific products or groups of products. It appears from the EEC-Treaty itself, that problems may arise. The establishment of average rates is allowed on the condition that the Commission shall issue appropriate directives or decisions, in case a Member State applies rates which are not in conformity with the national tax burden on (identical) products.

It is an unfortunate aspect of cumulative systems that remission and compensatory taxation can only take place in the form of averages that are approximated as well as possible. During the time of application of average rates many complaints were lodged concerning policies of fiscal dumping and protectionism.[35] Existing sentiments of distrust made a radical solution most desirable thereby resulting in the introduction of value added tax by the two Directives of 1967 and further harmonization by the Sixth Directive (*see* Chapter VIII *supra*). These directives provide for a uniform system of value added tax, involving the application to goods and services of a 'general tax on consumption' exactly proportional to the price of the goods and services, whatever the number of transactions which take place in the production and

---

34. Reugebrink, *op. cit.* note 16 *supra*, p. 134.
35. *See* K.V. Antal, 'Harmonisatie van de omzetbelasting in de Euro-markt', S. E. W. 1963, p. 12. However according to Rosendahl, *op. cit.* note 9 *supra*, p. 101, the averaging to determine estimated tax burdens is inevitably imprecise, 'it may have benefited the United States, since the averages tend to be on the conservative side and accordingly may result in lower border tax adjustments than might actually be justified'. Rosendahl admits that it is 'quite possible, given the differences in cascade tax burdens for integrated and non-integrated industries, that the tax charged on any particular product might be higher than paid on a similar domestic product by (integrated) domestic traders.'

distribution process before the stage at which tax is charged.[36] In such a system the tax burden can be exactly calculated, so that at least settlement at the borders should not cause any difficulties, that is with regard to distortion of competition.

The a-neutrality of cumulative cascade systems is not only a matter of competition. Tax frontiers also form a barrier to the free circulation of goods and thus interfere with balanced trade.[37] This interference is larger in a cumulative system, as will be seen in the next paragraph.

IX.3.2 Customs Borders

The earlier mentioned disadvantages resulting from the divergent sales tax systems made the Commission of the EC conclude that 'the tax frontiers' should be removed. The aim of abolishing such frontiers was explicitly proclaimed in the first two Directives of 1967 and in the Sixth Directive.[38] However, this conclusion does not necessarily follow from the provision itself on harmonization in the EEC-Treaty (Article 99). One could even deduce from this article that the internal tax frontiers will be maintained since harmonization is prescribed for turnover taxes, *including* compensatory measures in respect of trade between Member States.[39] It has been argued that only the methods of border tax adjustments are to be harmonized. Nevertheless, Article 99 does not exclude a removal of the tax frontiers altogether – in the future –.[40] The question is whether harmonization in itself will bring about the intended removal.

The conclusion of the Commission that the tax frontiers should be removed is not a necessary consequence of the requirement of harmonization. It is rather based on a misconception of (or lack of distinction between) tax frontiers and customs borders.

Customs borders are present whenever at the moment of and with regard to the crossing of a geographical (or political) border certain formalities have to be fulfilled.[41] These formalities may concern levying taxes or other charges, but also other measures may be taken, intended to influence the movement of goods across borders; such as quantitative restrictions and other measures

---

36. Dir. 67/227/EEC, Article 2.
37. This is apparent from the preamble to the EEC-Treaty, in which Member States recognize 'that the removal of existing obstacles calls for concerted actions in order to guarantee steady expansion, balanced trade and fair competition'.
38. *See* the preamble of Dir. 67/227 and 228/EEC and of Dir. 77/398/EEC.
39. *See* Antal, *op. cit.* note 35 *supra*, p. 19.
40. J. Reugebrink, *Omzetbelasting en EEG. Aspecten van een belasting over de toegevoegde waarde*, Deventer 1963, p. 19.
41. *Idem*, p. 20.

96

having equivalent effect.[42] In addition to this formalities can be concerned with other aspects, outside the field of customs law.

Tax frontiers and customs borders may coincide, however, this is not necessary. It seems obvious that the (compensatory) tax on importation and the remission on exportation take place at the moment when goods cross the geographical borders. This is especially so in cumulative cascade systems. The differentiation of tariffs inherent in such systems – one (high) rate would lead to unacceptable cumulation – makes physical inspection at the frontiers necessary in order to determine the applicable surcharge. This inspection forms a barrier to internal traffic in a customs union, which is based on the free circulation of goods. It is understandable that the attention of the Commission has been focused upon the settlement of indirect taxes at the borders. However, settlement may take place internally. Taxation of importation can take place at the importer, as if the tax were a domestic taxation. In case of this postponed accounting, inspection will take place based on the bookkeeping.[43] The customs borders – as regards VAT – will fall into disuse; however, the tax frontiers remain.[44]

Until recently, it was not at all clear what the Commission has meant with 'the tax frontiers'. From the directives for harmonization of the VAT it can be inferred that actually a removal of the customs borders has been the first intention. Measures of another magnitude are necessary for the actual removal of tax frontiers; these will be discussed under Chapters XI and XII.

IX.3.3 International Trade Complications

Complications in international trade stem from the multiplicity of sales tax systems. Not only adjustments at borders form a barrier, but also the protectionist tendencies in cumulative systems. One may question whether harmonization necessarily leads to the introduction of one single system of indirect taxation in the Member States of the European Community. A combination of systems is conceivable if these systems operate neutrally: the only choice, however, would be between non-cumulative systems.[45]

The Treaty of Rome does not prescribe one common system. Article 99 provides that the Commission shall consider how the turnover taxes may be harmonized. The Commission has opted for one common system. It is beyond doubt that one system will most effectively reduce to a minimum the trade barriers. An optimal situation will be created when existing tax frontiers are totally removed.

42. *Cfr.* Chapter VII.5 *supra.*
43. In a cumulative system the bookkeeping of importers has to meet very strict requirements.
44. *See further* on the postponed accounting system Chapter XI *infra.*
45. Antal, *op. cit.* note 35 *supra*, p. 14.

Before we turn to the subject of removal of tax barriers we will have a closer look at the place of delivery and service under the Sixth Directive.

IX.4 PLACE OF TAXABLE TRANSACTIONS UNDER THE SIXTH DIRECTIVE

Under the Sixth Directive subject to value added tax are:
1. the supplies of good or services effected for consideration within the territory of a country of a Member State by a taxable person as such, and
2. the importation of goods.

The levy of VAT is restricted to supplies effected *within the territory*. Thus the place of taxable transactions is essential in order to determine if, and which, national VAT law is applicable.

The question whether *supplies of goods* are effected within the territory of a Member State is closely connected with the concept of consumption in sales taxation. In Chapter II *supra*, it was argued that in sales taxation consumption has a specific meaning, which is related to the character of a sales tax namely as a general tax on consumption. In sales taxation a central place is given not to consumption, as an immediate event or as a more continuous process, but to the expenditure which makes the consumption possible. From a theoretical point of view the place where a good is purchased is most apparent for the determination of the place of expenditure. There and then the (trans)action relevant to VAT occurs. The 'adventures' of a product afterwards, whether it is actually ingested or used, or previous to that dispatched or transported, or even whether it is stolen or destroyed is in principle irrelevant.

Also the answer to the question whether *services* are supplied within the territory of a Member State is closely related to the concept of consumption in sales taxation. Services are consumed, where the person to whom they have been supplied 'enjoys' the service.[46] One should bear in mind that, like consumption, the expression 'enjoyment' bears its own connotation in sales taxation. Enjoyment does not equal 'economic use'. If this were not so, many services are not taxable since their 'economic use' is non existent or doubtful. As examples, consider faulty advice by a tax lawyer or unused designs by architects. This would be contrary to the theoretical starting-point: expenditure is consumption. The manner of consumption or the fact that no consumption occurs whatsoever is irrelevant. Thus 'useless' services are also 'consumed'. The identical criterion for consumption (or enjoyment) of services can be embraced as for consumption of goods: the purchase. It is suggested that for the determination of the place of taxation both for supplies of goods and of services this 'purchase-principle' will serve as a guideline.

---

46. *Cf.* J. Reugebrink, 'Het genot van een prestatie', W.F.R. 1961, p. 47. *See also* art. 9, par. 3b, of the Sixth Directive referring to the effective use and 'enjoyment' of services.

This principle, however, may encounter various problems in its realization. Therefore the Sixth Directive offers the following solutions for the place of the supply of goods (IX.4.1 *infra*) and for the place of the supply of services (IX.4.2 *infra*), which are not always in harmony with the proposed purchase-principle (or as it is with the legal character of the value added tax) but which were thought to reduce the application problems to a minimum, while still coming as close to the ideal as possible.

IX.4.1 *Place of Supply of Goods*

The problems regarding the place of supply of goods may best be illustrated by an example. Suppose an entrepreneur in Milano (Italy) supplies a car ordered by a client living in Amsterdam (the Netherlands). The car is transported from Milano to Amsterdam. In order to determine the place of transaction two alternatives present themselves. The supply takes place in Amsterdam or the supply is located in Milano. Supply in Amsterdam is in accordance with the legal character of a tax on consumption. Since the supply is purchased in Amsterdam, the sale is effected there, or in other words in Amsterdam the supply is enjoyed. This method of locating the transaction was considered problematic. The Italian supplier had to be subjected to Dutch value added tax. Theoretically this example should not necessarily cause problems, it is different however when the supplier is established for example in Seoul.

If on the contrary Milano is accepted as the place of transaction, various possibilities can be offered (provided double taxation or absence of taxation is to be avoided). The transaction is only subject to Italian VAT, a solution that requires a series of measures which at the time of the Sixth Directive were not acceptable yet. It should be noted that this solution in any case requires treating the import as a taxable event for deliveries located outside the Community like in the example of Seoul. Another possibility is: the delivery is subject to Italian VAT, however Italy remits the VAT upon exportation, (or subjects the delivery to zero-rating), the Netherlands charges VAT upon importation. At the time of introduction of the Sixth Directive this solution was considered the most acceptable among the Member States.[47] Such an arrangement can only be effective if within the EC the various national legislations regarding VAT are tuned to each other in order to avoid double

---

47. Obviously other possibilities can be thought of e.g. the supply is taxed in the Netherlands but the tax liability is deferred to the purchaser; or the delivery is taxed in Italy as well as the import is taxed in the Netherlands only the (positive) difference in tax rates between Italy and the Netherlands has to be paid; or the delivery in Italy is taxed and the 'use' in the Netherlands again only the difference in tax rates payable (*cf.* the American 'use-tax', Chapter XI.5.2 *infra*.) etc.

taxation and the absence of taxation. Article 8 of the Sixth Directive offers a general rule, in which a distinction is made between supplies of goods, which are dispatched or transported and other supplies. In the case goods are *not* dispatched or transported, the place of taxable transaction is where the goods are when the supply takes place. This rule clearly ties on to the purchase-principle. (*See* however for private consumers who dispatch a product *after* purchasing, and – thus after using it –, Section IX.4.1.1 *infra*.)

In case the goods are dispatched or transported, either by the supplier or by the person to whom they are supplied or by a third person, the place of taxable transaction is where the goods are at the time when the dispatch or transport to the person, to whom they are supplied begins. In case of exportation the VAT will be remitted, or the delivery will be subject to zero-rating. Upon importation into another Member State VAT will be charged. Theoretically, the place where the transporter delivers the goods to the person to whom they are supplied is more concordant with the purchase principle. However, the solution of the Sixth Directive has been guided by the desirability to avoid taxation of non-residents (in the example the Milanese supplier) in the distinct Member States. In general this tax would have been deductible at the person to whom the goods are supplied anyway. The arrangement of the Sixth Directive does not influence the final tax burden, but it was believed that many administrative obligations are avoided. The price to be paid however is existence of the tax frontiers between the Member States.

IX.4.1.1 Neutrality

Under Chapter III *supra* the concept of neutrality was introduced as a testing criterion of any given system of levying a sales tax. Neutrality is necessary among other things to prevent distortions of competition. The above mentioned solution for the place of supplies of goods guarantees this neutrality. Distortions, which could be caused by untaxed or double-taxed deliveries are avoided.[48] Only one situation causes severe distortions of neutrality. These distortions are related to purchases by private consumers.

As mentioned earlier (under Chapter II.3) application of the 'expenditure is consumption' concept conflicts with the principle of destination. Clearly, if the concept is fully continued, purchases by private consumers are taxed at the place and time of purchase. Even if a product is exported shortly after the

---

48. Possible distortions in cases of goods being installed or assembled by or on behalf of the supplier are avoided by the Sixth Directive, since in these cases the supply shall be deemed to be the place where the goods are installed. These distortions would be caused by the lower basis of assessment on import of the product not including the part of the consideration relating to the installation or assembling.

purchase, the immediate event from a theoretical point of view, has already taken place leaving no room for the country of destination principle. Up until a certain amount (namely the level of the traveler's exemption) the expenditure is indeed treated as an immediate event. Upon exportation no remittance is granted, upon importation no tax is levied either. In other words the principle of the country of origin is applied. For expenditures above the level of the traveler's exemption,[49] an outright exemption is made to the notion 'consumption is expenditure' and the principle of the country of destination prevails. The expenditure may be considered, as a fiction so to speak, to coincide with the intended (exportation and) importation.

Let us assume that the car in the given example is delivered to a private consumer in Milano. In cases in which this car is immediately transported by, or by order of, the consumer to the Netherlands, the delivery is taxable in Milano. But it will be zero-rated or a remittance will be granted. Upon importation into the Netherlands VAT is due. Thus by virtue of tax frontiers neutrality is safeguarded. Complications arise however when a product is not exported immediately after the purchase, but used at first and exported consequently. There will be no room for zero-rating or remittances (based on a fictitiously coinciding expenditure and importation). Thus when the car is not exported immediately upon the purchase, in Italy VAT will be levied, which will not be remitted even if the car is only used for a short period of time. In the Netherlands again VAT will be levied on account of the importation of an all but new car. Until recently the full amount of VAT was levied. Thus resulting, at least from the viewpoint of the consumer, in double taxation. In 1982 however, the Court of Justice of the EC ruled[50] that the VAT due upon importation should be reduced with the remainder of the VAT levied – and not deducted – in the Member State of exportation which is still included in the product at the moment of importation.[51]

IX.4.2 Place of Supply of Services

The problems regarding the place of supply of services are in principle not different from those caused by deliveries of goods. In the example (under IX.4) a small repair done to the car in Milano or advice given by a Milanese entrepreneur on how to convert the car could be taxable in Milano, even if the client is Dutch, just like the mentioned deliveries, followed by remittance and taxation upon importation. After the purchase of the service, 'export' of the service has to be assumed, followed by an official 'import' of the service.

49. At present 350 ECU.
50. Case 15/81 (Gaston Schul) 5 May 1982, E.C.R. 1982, p. 1409.
51. Till a maximum of VAT due on importation.

Within the EC another approach has been preferred, without settlements at the border. The place of the taxable supply is the sole decisive factor. Tax will be levied only once, neither remittances based on 'exportation' of services nor levies on occasion of 'importation' take place. For example the Sixth Directive situates the advice to convert the car, given by the Milanese entrepreneur, at Milano. Also the repair is struck, solely, by Italian VAT. Even when the advice or the repaired car will first be used in the Netherlands no Dutch VAT is levied. Ultimately the 'economic use' of both services is enjoyed in the Netherlands. From the viewpoint of consumption this is not objectionable, since it is in conformity with the purchase principle.

Theoretically this may be correct, however in practice in turns out that similar practices, located 'at home' – in case in the Netherlands – are taxed differently, since the tax rates are not harmonized between the Member States. Indeed it seems that the principle of the country of origin is prevailing. In the given examples it is. One should, however, bear in mind that entrepreneurs are entitled to a refund of the foreign tax – i.c. in Italy. Moreover under the Sixth Directive the principle of origin is accepted only for certain cases; generally the place of supply of services is formulated in such a way that the purchase-principle is applied leading to taxation in the country of actual use of the service. This however, has resulted in a rather extensive, if not complicated, regulation of the place of supply of services, in which neutrality is not always safeguarded, as proven by the given examples. (*See* for a more detailed description of the place of service under the Sixth Directive Chapter VIII.6.4 *supra*.)

The conclusion is that under the Sixth Directive border tax adjustments are a reality regarding the supply of goods. The supply of services is not bothered by tax barriers, as such, but the rules regarding this subject are complicated and do not always guarantee a neutral functioning of VAT in intra-Community transactions. Now we will turn to possibilities of removing tax barriers altogether.

Chapter X. The Removal of Tax Barriers; The Added Value Principle

X.1 INTRODUCTION

The settlement of sales taxes at the customs borders forms a barrier to international trade.[1] The formalities which have to be fulfilled signify delay and resulting expenses. According to the Commission of the EC the barriers to the free circulation of goods are caused by the maintenance of border tax adjustments. It has long been the intention of the Commission to eliminate these tax frontiers. In the motivation of the First and Sixth Directives one can find the following consideration:

'Whereas account should be taken of the objective of abolishing the imposition of tax on importation and the remission of tax on exportation in trade between Member States; whereas it should be ensured that the common system of turnover taxes is nondiscriminatory as regards the origin of goods and services, so that a common market permitting fair competition and resembling a real internal market may ultimately be achieved.'[2]

Until recently it was not very clear what is meant by this sentence. The phrase 'the objective of abolishing the imposition of tax on importation and the remission on exportation' has led to the conclusion that the destination principle will be abandoned insofar as it operates within the Community. Instead of the destination principle the principle of origin has been suggested to become the leading principle.[3] Actually a different principle is meant, namely the added value principle. In this chapter, it will be shown that this principle is incompatible with the legal character of an indirect general tax on consumption.

1. EEC reports on tax harmonization, IBFD Amsterdam 1964, p. 13.
2. Preamble, Directive 227/67/EEC, third motivation.
3. *See* for example R.W. Lindholm, 'Some Value Added Tax Impacts on the International Competitiveness of Producers', *Journal of Finance* 1968, p. 660.

The most plausible approach is the removal of tax barriers, maintaining the destination principle. In 1985 the European Commission published a White Paper offering proposals to remove the tax barriers within the Community, we will deal with these proposals under Chapters XI and XII.

X.2 ADDED VALUE PRINCIPLE

The origin principle assumes that goods will be taxed where they are produced, regardless of where they are eventually consumed. On the other hand the destination principle taxes products where they are consumed, regardless of where they were originally produced. The value added tax, especially when it extends to the retail stage, does not fit neatly into the principle of origin.[4] Where value added tax applies to the final retail stage, goods will necessarily be taxed in the country where they are consumed, that is the country of destination.[5] If one wants to apply the origin principle, so that no border tax adjustments would be necessary, difficulties arise in regard to imported products. These problems are caused by the inevitable[6] deduction of credit for input tax. The natural result would be the allocation of the tax between the countries concerned in proportion to the value added in each.[7] This allocation of tax according to where the value is created is called the added value principle or the restricted origin principle.[8]

An example may clarify this principle: Suppose that a product is manufactured in country X and exported to country Y, where it is finished and sold to the final consumer. The value added in each country is 100, in each country the tax rate is 10 per cent. The tax paid in country X will be $100 \times 10 \% = 10$. The tax paid in country Y will be $200 \times 10 \% = 20$, less deduction of credit for input tax $10 = 10$. In each country the added value is equally taxed; the yield of taxation is equally divided.

The situation changes if the tax rates are different, say 20 per cent in country X. The tax paid in country X will be 100×20 per cent $= 20$. The tax paid in country Y will be 200×10 per cent $= 20$, less deduction of credit for input tax $20 = 0$. (If the rate in country X is still higher a refund will have to be given for the tax paid in X.)

---

4. A.J. Easson, *Tax Law and Policy in the EEC*, London 1980, p. 101.
5. *Idem.*
6. Without deduction of credit for input tax a cumulative system would be the result.
7. Easson, *op. cit.* note 4 *supra*, p. 101.
8. The added value principle has been advocated by D. Biehl, *Ausfuhrland-Prinzip, Einfuhrland-Prinzip und gemeinsamer Markt-Prinzip. Ein Beitrag zur Theorie der Steuerharmonisierung*, Köln 1968. Charles E. McLure, Jr., refers to the restricted origin principle: 'State and Federal Relations in the Taxation of Value Added', *The Journal of Corporation Law* 1980, pp. 127–139.

Although in each country the added value is taxed, the yield of taxation is not in conformity with the value added in each country. From the given examples it can be seen that application of the added value principle ensures that the tax burden in the importing country (Y) remains equal, regardless whether the exporting country applies a different tax rate. The tax is neutral since the domestic products are equally taxed. In as far as the exporting country (X) is concerned different tax rates have no effect; tax is paid, on the value added, according to that country's rate. Only the importing country is affected by differences in tax rates. Imports from a higher tax country result in a reduction in revenue – caused by the deduction of credit for input tax –.[9]

If the method was employed that the total amount of value added tax is calculated based on the appropriate rates in the countries where the value is added (the base-on-base method) this would be neutral as regards the allocation of tax revenue.[10] Each country would receive the appropriate tax on the domestically added value, however, the consumers prices would be affected, if tax rates were different.[11]

For these problems, basically caused by different tax rates, various solutions have been suggested.

In the first place, one could do nothing on the assumption that products may equally well be imported from low-tax countries as from high-tax countries. The pertaining gains and losses will largely cancel each other out.[12] However, this can not be assumed with absolute certainty. Moreover, the fact that the tax is neutral both for the importer and the final consumer (the tax burden is the same on products from low-tax countries as from high-tax countries) does not preclude that more products are imported from a high-tax country.[13] Since in countries with high indirect taxes, the direct taxes can be lower.[14] This may affect production costs and therefore the competition. Thus imports from high-tax countries might be more attractive, causing a reduction in revenue for the importing country.

In the second place, a so-called 'butoir' could be instituted. The reduction in revenue caused by the higher rates applied in the exporting country can be parried by a restriction of the tax credit in the importing country to the rate of tax applied there.[15] Without further measures the neutrality will be affected: a different tax burden will result in different consumer prices of products with

9. Easson, *op. cit.* note 4 *supra*, p. 102. Imports from a lower tax country cause an increase in revenue.
10. In other words the subtractive method. (*See* Chapter V.4.1 *supra*.)
11. Easson, *op. cit.* note 4 *supra*, p. 102.
12. *Idem.*
13. *Idem.*
14. J. Reugebrink, 'Directe en indirecte belastingen: een achterhaalde classificatie?' p. 145 in *Cijns en Dijns*, Deventer 1975.
15. Easson, *op. cit.* note 4 *supra*, p. 102.

the same added value. It has been suggested that the exporting country should refund the balance to the retailer, in order to lift this distortion of neutrality.[16] The reasoning is that the exporting country should not object to this, since under the present destination principle it now refunds the entire amount of tax which it has received. Of course, this reasoning is false. Under the destination principle the refund can be set against a full taxation of the imports! Application of a 'butoir', in order to save the added value principle,[17] leads to the result that high-tax countries always lose on it. Further considerable administrative complexities make application of a 'butoir' unattractive. It would be more simple to refund upon exportation all the tax levied but then the added value principle will be abandoned. Apart from a 'butoir' other solutions can be imagined.

The allocation of the tax which has taken place automatically in the exporting country, since no remission is given of the tax on exportation, can be corrected by a system of accounting and compensation.[18] In the example above Member State Y levying a tax at 10 per cent will end up empty handed if the rate in Member State X is 20 per cent. For compensation – 10 per cent × 100 – Member State Y will have to turn to export-State X. It is clear that a fairly high level of administrative efficiency and of cooperation between tax-authorities is necessary. By this system of compensation at least the customs borders will be removed. It should be noticed, however, that the added value principle is (partially) abandoned.

Another solution might be the adoption of a single common rate of tax for all transactions prior to the retail stage.[19] The Member States are free to fix their own rates applicable to the final stage. This solution would rather complicate the national systems. Neither should the common rate be too low, to avoid tax fraud in the retail stage.[20] In addition, compensation remains necessary when exemptions are introduced and reduced rates are applied in the retail stage.[21] This is again accompanied by the administrative burden between the Member States. Even when this administrative burden is considered acceptable, objections against the added value principle can be raised of both practical and fundamental nature.

A practical objection is the possible growth of cross-border shopping.[22] This problem is more easily mentioned than quantified. The macro-economic

16. *Idem*.
17. The added value principle will be saved only partially.
18. Easson, *op. cit.* note 4 *supra*, p. 106.
19. *Idem*.
20. The avoidance of fraud has been one of the reasons for introduction of a (multi-stage) VAT-system instead of a (one-stage) sales tax. *See* Chapter VIII.2 *supra*.
21. Which may be expected considering the (efforts to reduce the) regressive effects. *See* Chapter VI.3 *supra*.
22. This objection can also be raised when the customs borders are removed under application of the destination principle without unification or approximation of rates.

effects may be negligible while the losses in frontier areas suffered by retailers whose businesses are located there may be substantial. When all physical inspection at the borders is removed, which is the case under the added value principle, an appreciable loss in revenue for a Member State can be expected when the rates in neighboring Member States differ significantly. An advantage could be that this may lead to a degree of 'enforced' harmonization.[23]

An objection of fundamental nature against the added value principle is based on the legal character of a general indirect tax on consumption. Before we turn to this subject under X.3., the possibility of the *unification* of rates will be mentioned.[24] Actually, it has been suggested that an approximation will be sufficient, since increased transportation costs will permit some divergence without undue distortion.[25]

At first sight a uniform rate could offer the solution to all the problems posed. Between (the Member) States applying a common VAT system, the tax will benefit the country where the value has been added. Between the Member States no refunds will be necessary. The tax frontiers seem to be removed. Distortions of competition, like those between countries applying different rates, are not possible. Nevertheless, fundamental objections can be raised against application of the added value principle even when uniform rates are applied.

X.3 THE ADDED VALUE PRINCIPLE AND THE BENEFIT PRINCIPLE

Without unification of rates the removal of tax frontiers, based on the application of the added value principle, causes distortion of competition and diversion of international trade. The removal of tax frontiers by means of the added value principle while rates are unified also raises objections notwithstanding the advantages previously outlined.

In the first place, if the tax will benefit the country where the value has been added, this procedure is, in my view, contrary to the legal character of an indirect tax on consumption. The legal character of the value added tax permitting destination taxation (*see supra* Chapter II.4), can be viewed from the following. VAT, like most sales taxes, has little to do with ability to pay. It can hardly be used as a tool of redistribution of wealth. From this no arguments can be derived in favor or against the destination or added value principle. It has been argued (under Chapter II.4 *supra*) that the indirect character leads to the application of the destination principle. This is sanc-

---

23. Easson, *op. cit.* note 4 *supra*, p. 108, uses the term 'spontaneous harmonization'.
24. Easson, p. 103.
25. A difference of 3 points has been suggested as acceptable. B. Veenhof, 'Fiscale Harmonisatie: de communautaire doeleinden en hun gevolgen voor de Lid-Staten', WFR 1973, p. 95.

tioned by international rules. In my view the guiding principle to choose in favor of the country of destination is the so called *benefit principle*. According to this principle the choice between consumption and production as the basis of taxation should depend on the nature of the goods and services provided by the public sector.[26] Under this principle, an origin based tax is only justifiable if public services were primarily supportive of productive activities. It can hardly be assumed that goods and services subject to a general indirect tax on *consumption*, in a given country are taxed primarily in relation with production, so that based on a (restricted) origin principle – namely the added value principle – goods and services may carry a tax burden upon exportation. If the consumers are primarily the beneficiaries of the government services which the VAT finances, they should bear the full burden of these taxes in their own country.[27] It is therefore suggested that taxes on consumption of private consumers should exclusively benefit the country in which the expenditure takes place, the country of destination.

In the second place, the fact that application of the value added principle with uniform rates excludes the risk of distortion in the conditions of competition, does not mean that application of the added value principle will have no consequences at all as regards the Revenue of the Member States.

Countries with a negative balance of external trade will suffer a budgetary loss.[28] Although the tax on exportation, as contrasted with the destination principle, will benefit the Revenue, the tax on importation is omitted. These problems are caused by the 'hybrid' character of VAT. VAT is basically a 'European tax',[29] however, the continuing existence of national Revenues, as regards the yield of the VAT, makes this tax the same as many 'national' taxes. Apportionment of the tax to the country of the added value would not conflict with the legal character of a tax on consumption if the European Community were one 'country of destination'.[30] This would only be the case if one Treasury were instituted, benefiting from the collected VAT. Budgetary losses would then be impossible, since the Member States would have become one tax territory, at least as regards VAT. This has not been intended by the EEC-Treaty. We will turn now to the proposals of the Commission published in the White Paper in which the destination principle is fully upheld.

---

26. R. Musgrave and P.B. Musgrave, *Public Finance in Theory and Practice*, New York 1973, p. 187. *See also* McLure, *op. cit.* note 8 *supra*, p. 133. and R.W. Rosendahl, *Border Tax Adjustments: Problems and Proposals, Law and Policy in International Business* 1970, p. 91.
27. Rosendahl, *op. cit.* note 26 *supra*, p. 91.
28. As contrasted with the destination principle.
29. *Cf.* Chapter VIII, *supra*.
30. J. Reugebrink, *Omzetbelasting*, Deventer 1973, p. 37.

Chapter XI. The Removal of Tax Barriers; White Paper from the Commission to the European Council

XI.1 INTRODUCTION

On 29 June 1985, the Commission published a White Paper[1] for the European Council with the aim of working out in more detail a program and timetable in order, within the Community, to 'achieve a single large market by 1992 thereby creating a more favorable environment for stimulating enterprise, competition and trade'.

The White Paper is not intended to cover every possible issue which affects the integration of the economies of the Member States of the Community. It focuses on the Internal Market and the measures which are directly necessary to achieve a single integrated market embracing the 320 million people of the enlarged Community. The measures that need to be taken have been classified in the White Paper under three headings:
- Part I: the removal of physical barriers;
- Part II: the removal of technical barriers;
- Part III: the removal of tax barriers.

The detailed timetable for implementing the measures is to be found in the Annex to the White Paper.

In what follows, the content of each part is first summarized and then the third part – the removal of tax barriers – is discussed; in addition an alternative system (a clearing system without clearing) will be suggested.

XI.2 THE REMOVAL OF PHYSICAL BARRIERS

XI.2.1 General

The customs posts at the borders are the most obvious examples of physical

---

1. 'Completing the Internal Market', White Paper from the Commission to the European Council, COM (85) 310 final, 55 pp. Annex: timetable for Completing the Internal Market by 1992, 32 pp. This Chapter has previously been published in *Intertax* 1987/6.

barriers. Barriers, immigration control, passports and the (occasional) searching of personal baggage are to the ordinary citizen the clearest manifestation of the continued division of the Community. These barriers are equally important to trade and industry, commerce and business.[2]

The Commission's objective is to simplify existing procedures and ultimately to do away with internal frontier controls in their entirety. The Commission recognizes, however, that certain national protective measures do not in all their aspects fall within the scope of the Treaty, e.g. measures against terrorism and the illicit trade in drugs. If the objective of abolishing all internal frontier controls is to be met, alternative means of protection will need to be found.

Obvious examples, in the Commission's opinion, are improving controls at the external frontiers of the Community, using spot checks at the internal frontiers and inland, and further enhancing cooperation between the national authorities concerned.

The considerations which apply to goods and individuals are examined separately.

XI.2.2 Control of Goods

The principles of proportionality and non-discrimination have hitherto been central to the attempt to make internal frontier formalities more flexible and to simplify the free movement of goods. These principles will continue to apply in the future. Initially, the Commission intends to achieve greater flexibility at the frontiers by, for instance, avoiding duplication of controls on both sides of the frontier ('banalisation').

The shift from the alleviation to the elimination of internal frontier controls, however, is a major step and requires a qualitatively different approach. The Commission makes a distinction here between measures in the field of commercial and economic policy, health controls, transport checks and the collection of statistics.

As regards commercial and economic policy, the Commission takes the view that it is not an unreasonable aim to achieve this abolition of national and regional quotas by 1992. The most important objectives are that Article 115 of the EEC Treaty should no longer be applicable and that (by automatically adjusting agricultural prices) recourse to Article 46 should be removed.

Under this Article, monetary compensatory amounts can be applied to imports and exports.

2. *In – en Uitvoernieuws* (Import and Export News) 1983, p. 219, states that 'settling of formalities in the European Community . . ., according to Dutch sources in Brussels, costs fl. 3.650 million a year. This is the equivalent of 5.7 per cent of the price of all goods carried by road'.

As regards health protection, internal frontier posts are often used for making veterinary and plant health checks. The Commission intends initially that these controls (and the issuing of certificates) will have to be made exclusively at the place of departure. Subsequently, by aligning national standards to common standards for veterinary and plant health, the role of certificates should be drastically reduced. Specific restrictions should then only be necessary in emergencies such as epidemics.

As regards transport, it is intended, inter alia, to do away with quotas and introduce common safety standards.

As regards statistics, modern methods of data collection, including sampling techniques, can ensure that accurate and comprehensive trade statistics are compiled without the need for frontier formalities.

As regards the timetable, the Commission recommends that work should be planned in two stages. In the first stage – where possible by 1988 – the emphasis should be to shift controls and formalities away from the internal frontiers.

In the second stage, barriers and controls at the internal frontiers should be eliminated in their entirety by 1992.

XI.2.3 Control of Individuals

The formalities affecting individual travelers are, firstly, police checks relating to the identity of the person concerned and the safety of personal effects being carried. Secondly, tax checks are carried out with regard to personal effects being carried (see XI.4.3).

In addition to proposals concerning the introduction of a common passport and the Green Disc, the Commission intends, in the short term, to seek a commitment from the Member States that no new or more stringent controls or formalities affecting individuals are introduced at internal frontiers. An attempt will be made to strengthen controls at external frontiers and enhance cooperation between the relevant national authorities.

Proposals for directives will also be drawn up concerning policy with regard to the issuing of visas and the granting of asylum, and the approximation of arms and drugs legislation.[3]

---

3. The Commission does not say whether and to what extent the proposals on drug trafficking will also reflect the differences in approach as regards prosecution and punishment.

XI.3 THE REMOVAL OF TECHNICAL BARRIERS

XI.3.1 General

The Commission states that the elimination of border controls, important as it is, does not of itself create a genuine common market. Goods and people moving within the Community should not find obstacles inside the Member States as opposed to meeting them at the border. Examples of technical barriers are the various requirements imposed by the Member States on products as regards health and safety or with a view to protecting the environment or consumers. Only when these barriers have been removed will the Community be in a position to create the large economic and industrial market which will enable companies to achieve economies of scale and improve their competitive position.

The Commission's own general strategy is aimed more at mutual recognition and equivalence than at harmonization.

The approximation of the Member States' Laws, regulations and administrative provisions, in accordance with Article 100 of the EEC Treaty, will however be continued.

The Commission is trying to limit the harmonization of legislation to the establishment of basic requirements.[4] Clearly, action under Article 100 will be quicker and more effective if the Council were to agree not to allow the unanimity requirement to obstruct progress.

XI.3.2 Technical Barriers

After outlining the strategy (described above), the White Paper goes on to discuss the following aspects in turn: public procurement, free movement for labor and the professions, a common market for services, capital movements, the creation of suitable conditions for industrial cooperation, and the application of Community law.

As regards public procurement, the authorities concerned still tend to keep their purchases and contracts within their own country. The public procurement market, it is announced, will be opened up by means of Directives.

The Commission considers it crucial that the obstacles within the Community to free movement for the self-employed and employees be removed by 1992.

Among other things, the comparability of vocational training qualifications

---

4. Article 155 of the EEC Treaty expressly provides for the possibility of delegation. This opens the way for a simplified legislative procedure, which has already been applied successfully in customs matters, *see* Chapter VII, note 46.

should ultimately result in the introduction of a 'vocational training card'.

In the Commission's view, it is no exaggeration to see the establishment of a common market in services as one of the main preconditions for a return to economic prosperity. The Commission is planning quickly to put forward proposals[5] which open up the international market in the traditional service sectors, notably banking, insurance and transport. As regards the new services sectors, too, such as information and data processing, marketing and audio-visual services, proposals can be expected in the short term regarding, inter alia, a single Community-wide broadcasting area and electronic banking.

The liberalization of capital movements is not needed only in order to remove barriers to the free movement of goods, services and persons; monetary stability is also an essential condition of the proper operation and developments of the internal market. In addition, the opening up of the capital and money market will provide a stimulus for the development of the Community.

Within the framework of the existing safeguard clauses in the EEC Treaty (Articles 73 and 108), the Commission is trying to ensure that, from 1992 onwards, any residual currency control measures should be applied by means other than border controls.

The Commission sees the creation of a legal framework facilitating cooperation between enterprises and principally involving the coordination of company law and the harmonization of legislation on intellectual and industrial property (e.g. by introducing the Community trade mark).

A White Paper on the taxation of enterprises is promised for the end of 1985! Unfortunately this Paper has not yet been published.

The chapter on technical barriers is rounded off with a short survey of the application of Community law. The majority of complaints about infringement of Community law relates to Articles 30 to 36 of the EEC Treaty – quantitative restrictions and measures having equivalent effect – (*see* Chapter VII Section 5 *supra*). Because of a lack of resources, the Commission can only settle fewer than half these cases. As well as improving and rationalizing its internal procedures, the Commission will have to take more systematic action, i.e. by publishing general communications setting out the legal situation (particularly in regard to Articles 30 to 36) for the whole of an economic sector.[6]

If the above policy options are realized, the customs' main task will still be to supervise the remaining operation of the indirect taxation system applying in the Member State concerned. For the customs, therefore, the problem of

5. *See* Annex (pp. 25–28): for most of the proposals, the target date for adoption by the Council is 1987.
6. The Commission intends to publish communications on cars, foodstuffs, pharmaceuticals and chemicals by 1988.

doing away with physical controls coincides largely with the removal of tax barriers. This is the problem that we now have to examine.

XI.4 THE REMOVAL OF TAX BARRIERS

XI.4.1 General

After summarizing the historical development of the VAT Directives and draft Directives and of the excise (draft) Directives, the Commission states that the harmonization of indirect taxation has always been regarded as an essential and integral part of achieving a true Common Market. However, in recent years, momentum has been lost.

If, the Commission continues, goods and services and people are to move freely from one Member State to another 'in just the same way as they can within a Member State', it is essential that frontier controls be abolished. Given the relationship between prices and levels of taxation (i.e. of VAT and excise duties), we need to consider whether it would be practically possible, in the absence of frontier controls, for Member States to charge significantly different levels of indirect taxation. A distinction is made between commercial traffic and the individual traveler.

XI.4.2 Commercial Traffic

The starting point for the Commission is the 14th VAT Directive[7] and the system of postponed accounting which shifts the accounting procedures for VAT from frontiers to inland tax offices. In view of the experience gained in the Benelux,[8] the Commission thinks there are no convincing reasons why the Directive has not (yet) been adopted by the Council. Adoption of the Directive will not, however, result in the complete abolition of frontier controls. The Commission advocates the setting up of a Community 'Clearing House System' to ensure that VAT collected in the exporting Member State and deducted in the importing Member State is reimbursed to the latter on a bilateral basis.[9]

However, the Commission foresees problems in the present widely diver-

---

7. *See* D.B. Bijl, 'Draft 13th and 14th Council Directives relating to turnover taxes', WFR 1982, p. 127. *et seq.*
8. And, earlier, in Ireland and the United Kingdom, where moreover the postponed accounting system has since been abolished.
9. *See* A.L.C. Simons, 'Simplification of VAT Procedures in Intra-Community Trade', *Intertax* 1981/10, p. 375 *et seq. See also* B.J.M. Terra, *Omzetbelasting bij grensoverschrijdend verkeer* (Turnover tax at cross-border traffic), FED Deventer 1984, Chapter IV.

gent rates and coverage of VAT which would expose the system to heavy and systematic fraud and evasion.

It would be all too easy for traders in high-rate Member States to obtain supplies from low-rate Member States and omit them from their records.

The Clearing House System could neither provide a solution for the small trader not registered for VAT, who could legitimately shop across the border and would do so (according to the Commission) where significant differences in taxation and corresponding differences in prices existed.

The Commission concludes that there is no means of removing the frontier controls (and thus the frontiers) if there are significant tax and corresponding price differences between the Member States.

In addition, as regards excise duties, the normal commercial transactions (removal from the bonded warehouse, transit,[10] delivery to a warehouse in the Member State of destination) require frontier controls.

The first simplification which the Commission proposes is for the Council to adopt the Directives on common structures for excises which are already before it; a further streamlining could be achieved by linking national systems of excise suspension.

The present great differences in excise taxation would, however, (if they persisted) lead to fraud and evasion. The conclusion is that a considerable adjustment is needed in excise coverage (and, hence, in the number of duties) and rates.

XI.4.3 Individual Traveler

The Commission's 'analysis' concentrates, as regards both VAT and excise duties, on the fact that differences in tax levels result in considerable differences in prices. They create a powerful incentive for people living in high-rate countries to cross the border and shop in low-tax countries. The existence of travelers' allowances, their modest amounts[11] and the disproportionate difficulty in obtaining agreement to limited increases all demonstrate, according to the Commission, that it would be impossible to dismantle tax frontiers unless there were a considerable measure of approximation of indirect taxation.

XI.4.4 Approximation

In the Commission's opinion, 'complete harmonization, which has come to

---

10. The White Paper, in our opinion, is wrong to use the word 'import'.
11. 350 ECU.

imply absolute identity in every respect, is not essential' and for this reason we should now use the term 'approximation'.

The Commission refers to the situation in the United States, where there are no tax frontiers as such, and differences of up to 5 per cent even between neighboring states are acceptable. On this basis, it is argued that if a target rate is introduced by the Community, the margin at either side of that rate should be +/− 2 ½ per cent.

'Purely as an illustration,' this would mean that, if the norm for the standard rate were 16 1/2 per cent, actual rates adopted by Member States could be in the range of 14 to 19 per cent. In the case of excises the indicative range of +/− 2 ½ per cent would be less significant as excises frequently account for a large proportion of the retail price.

The Commission admits that further study is needed and confines itself in the White Paper to a general discussion of the broad picture. A survey of total revenue from indirect taxation as a percentage of GDP shows that for most Member States the total yield differs little from the Community average (10.68 per cent).[12]

According to the Commission, approximation, looked at in this way, 'presents a manageable budgetary problem for most Member States and it would not seriously disturb the existing relationship between direct and indirect taxation'.

The problem, therefore, is not so much the total yield of indirect taxation but the composition of that yield, the division between VAT and excises.

Given adequate time, flexibility and political will, approximation will cause no more difficulty than many Member States have encountered in determining their domestic tax policy.

XI.4.4.1 VAT

The approximation of VAT focuses on three areas:
  (i) the common base;
  (ii) the number of rates; and
  (iii) the level of the rate or rates, and particularly of the standard rate.
As regards the common base, the Commission recommends that the current draft Directives (eight in all) be adopted.

It also announces three further proposals.[13]

The remaining derogations to the common base (food, second-hand goods, fuel and transport) will have to be tackled in subsequent proposals. As far as

---

12. Weighted average for the Community, excluding Greece, where the requisite data were not available.
13. On small business, flat rate farmers and passenger transport.

the number of rates is concerned, the Commission finds that 'despite the present predominance of multiple-rate systems, there are strong arguments in favor of a single rate'. A standard rate of 16 1/2 per cent is again given as an illustration.

In anticipation of a decision about rates of tax, the Commission has put forward a 'standstill' proposals, whereby an increase in the number of VAT rates in the Member States or in the levels of the various rates is excluded.[14]

Coupled with the Clearing House System mentioned above, the approximation of rates would make the removal of tax barriers by the end of 1992 a reality! (*See* for further development, Chapter XII *infra*.)

XI.4.4.2 Excises

To begin with, the Directives on the common structure of excises should be adopted. Subsequently, according to the Commission, VAT and excises should be treated together when proposals for common rates are drawn up. This is bound up with the fact that high VAT yields often exist side by side with low excise yields, and *vice versa*. Proposals for maximum and minimum rates, to be put forward at the same time as those on VAT rates, will need to be accompanied by a 'standstill', whereby Member States would undertake to avoid moving away from the common bands.

Finally, the Commission recognizes that the approximation of indirect taxation will give rise to considerable problems for some Member States and that as a consequence it may be necessary to provide for derogations, although these should be kept to a minimum.

XI.5 REMOVAL OF TAX BARRIERS; ANALYSIS

XI.5.1 General

The central question in the abolishment of tax barriers[15] is: how far is it possible without frontier controls (and possibly also without cross-border

---

14. *See* the proposal of 21 November 1985, COM (85) 606 final, which has since been published: O.J. 1985, C 313. In view of the follow up given to the White Paper (*See* Chapter XII *infra*) the proposal has been withdrawn.
15. I confine myself to indirect taxes, although I realize that it is *direct* taxes which can play a crucial role in the completion of the internal market. Despite the Commission's assertion that the ratio of direct to indirect taxation does not seriously need to be altered, we find that Member States with an average revenue from indirect taxes lower than the weighted Community average can in general manage successfully with the standard rate (or rates).

In Member States whose average revenue is considerably higher than the weighted average, 'approximation' will have to result in an increase in direct taxes. If at all possible, the resulting increase in market prices and a disadvantageous export position may give rise to further (serious) distortions in commercial traffic between Member States.

taxable transactions) to levy indirect taxes which are still tailored as closely as possible to the economic and tax situations of the different Member States?

Various distinctions are drawn by the Commission in this connection. First, there is the difference between commercial traffic and the individual traveler. Another difference concerns the structure of the taxes in question, i.e. VAT and excise duties.

A third distinction is the one drawn between measures that can be taken in the short term and those which can be accomplished only in the longer term.

The difference between *commercial traffic* and the *individual traveler* is significant, since it seems that schemes are possible in the former case – notably as regards VAT – which will allow a substantial reduction in and even the removal of tax barriers without infringing the country of destination principle (tax is charged where the consumption occurs).

` In this respect, there is still room, too, for (a degree of) national differentiation as regards rates and the total tax burden.

As regards the individual traveler, the simplification and ultimately, the removal of frontier formalities seems possible only if the country of origin principle is accepted, i.e. tax is charged in the country where the consumer expenditure occurs. It seems that the adverse effect thereof can only be contained (and made acceptable to the national economies) if rates and tax burdens are reconciled or harmonized.

The difference between *VAT and excise duties* has a bearing on the possibilities, particularly as regards commercial traffic, of reducing or abolishing frontier formalities.

Such possibilities depend on the number of charges which the collection system for the particular indirect tax involves. In the case of VAT, these are (imports excluded) all transactions of traders, with the exception of exempt trades, farmers who qualify for the agricultural scheme and certain small traders. Despite these exceptions, this means a considerably broader tax base than is the case with excises, where, in principle, in addition to importers, only manufacturers of the excise goods concerned are affected by the collection system.[16]

The difference between arrangements to be made in the *short term* and those which can be introduced only in the *longer term* is of particular interest in connection with the proposals being put forward on VAT. That is, in the short term, the introduction of a postponed accounting system, as set out in the proposal for a 14th Directive, and, in the longer term, the introduction of the Clearing House System. In my opinion, the interesting difference between

16. In addition, most excise acts still recognize excise-suspension schemes to a greater or lesser extent; under such schemes dealers also take part in the charging system – in the Netherlands, for example, this is the case in particular with the excises on mineral oils and alcohol – but the schemes are not compulsory for commerce and a trader can choose to stay outside such a scheme.

postponed accounting and the Clearing House System is that whereas the former tries to reduce or even remove frontier formalities while maintaining the taxable event of importation and, hence, cancellation at the export stage (zero rate), the latter abandons both taxing and cancellation.

XI.5.2 THE CROSS-BORDER MOVEMENT OF GOODS AND TAXES ON CONSUMPTION

A feature of indirect taxes is that they are not levied at the stage where the burden is intended to rest. Taxes on consumption, for instance, are levied at the production and/or distribution stage, i.e. prior to consumption.

The lag between levy and consumption, or rather consumer expenditure, is greatest in systems involving a single levy at the production stage. In the Netherlands this is the case at present with excises and the special taxes on consumption. However, even a general consumption tax such as the turnover tax can be levied in this way, as was the Dutch turnover tax in the 1930s. In countries where tax is still levied in this way today, e.g. India, the term 'general excise' is used. Within such systems, in addition to levying tax at the production stage it is also still necessary to levy tax on the importation of goods (and conversely, to repay tax when they are exported).

With systems where the lag between the levy and the consumption is shorter or even non-existent, it would seem less important to include the importation of goods in the taxation. This is most clearly shown in the system involving only one levy at the distribution stage, i.e. retailing. One is re-minded here of the Sales Tax levied by different States (and many cities) in the USA. Taxable event and consumption expenditure are thus two aspects of one transaction.

Such taxes can be seen notably in situations where a levy at the importation stage is simply not possible. Yet there may also be a need to include imports in such a system, namely when the consumer spends outside the region where taxation takes place. In the United States, an effort is being made to tax relatively large amounts of expenditure in such cases with a 'use tax'.[17]

As regards systems involving several stages in the levying, a distinction should be made between cumulative and non-cumulative types (*see* Chapters IV and V *supra*).

With the former kind, such as was the basis of Dutch turnover tax legisla-tion between 1940 and 1969, a levy on the importation of goods, even in commercial traffic, was necessary merely in order to make up again for the taxation 'missed' prior to the actual importation into the Netherlands. For these reasons it was not just the manufacturer's rate which was charged in

---

17. *See* e.g. R.W. Lindholm, *Value Added Tax and Other Tax Reforms*, Chicago, 1976, 94 pp. *et seq.*

respect of imports: a detailed system of 'import surcharges' was applied in order to raise the tax burden to the level (resulting partly from cumulation) for comparable goods available internally.

With non-cumulative systems, such a 'recouping maneuver' is not usually necessary, especially if the system already has its own inbuilt 'recouping effect', as is the case with a Value Added Tax which – like the 'Community' version – is levied in accordance with the 'invoice' system (the 'tax credit' method). One may even wonder – as indeed happened in the Netherlands before 1969 – whether, in such a system, the taxable event of importation cannot be left out in respect of commercial traffic. The possible objection that there are also situations where entrepreneurs have no or only a partial right to deduct does not necessarily mean that taxing the importation is the only solution for this problem. Of course, if relatively few of the total number of importations are involved, all this could also be settled by some other means e.g. by the so-called 'integration levy', as also occurs in respect of own manufactures which are not eligible for (complete) deduction.[18]

The value and significance of the taxable event of importation of goods are of course discussed further in what follows, with regard to both commercial traffic and the individual passenger. At this point, one is reminded that the import and export of *services* is usually not included: (at any rate) in the Community's VAT system, there is no mention of such a taxable event. It is more appropriate that the country where tax can be levied most efficiently is the place of service.[19]

In other words, it is the service itself which is taxed as such, and not – as in the case of goods – the importation as a specially taxable event. The reason for this difference is historical, but is perhaps influenced too by the fact that customs officers so seldom encounter the cross-border provision of services.

XI.5.3 HISTORY OF THE POSTPONED ACCOUNTING SYSTEM IN THE NETHERLANDS

In the Netherlands the postponed accounting system was introduced in 1966. It was contained in the Special Regulations III Order relating to the Turnover Tax Act of 1954; the reduction of frontier formalities was already envisaged in it. To that effect, as is the case with the current system under Article 23 of the 1968 Turnover Tax Act,[20] entrepreneurs who *regularly* obtained goods from abroad (at that time, Belgium and Luxembourg) could be included. The original system did not just involve postponing the levy of turnover tax, but

18. The so-called 'self-supply', *see* Article 3(1)(h) of the Dutch Turnover Tax Act 1968 and Article 5(7)(a) of the Sixth Directive on turnover taxes.
19. In principle, the place where the service is purchased. For this 'purchase principle' *see supra* Chapter IX.4.
20. Based on Article 23 of the Sixth Directive.

also meant that, when a person crossed the internal (Benelux) border, he could make an oral declaration and then send in his own statement to the Central Statistical Office. This last feature, in particular, together with the complicated rate structure of the time (including the import surcharges mentioned in Section 5.2 before) meant that in practice the system was never very highly regarded.

The major breakthrough as regards postponed accounting came with the introduction of VAT. The system was restricted to postponement of the import declaration to the periodic internal VAT return, but extended to cover *all* imports. The simplicity of VAT is a further advantage: the same rates apply to imports as they do internally, and there are no import surcharges which made collection under a cumulative system so complicated.

XI.5.3.1 The Significance of the Postponed Accounting System

The most striking advantage of the postponed accounting system is, of course, the simplification of import formalities. In addition, such system – at any rate as it exists in the Benelux countries and as it has been proposed (in compulsory form) in the 14th draft Directive – achieves a *better balance* between taxation on importation and internal taxation.

When goods are supplied internally, tax is paid by the supplier and deducted by the purchaser in principle at the same time, i.e. in the returns of both parties relating to the same period, that of duly invoicing. When tax is levied in accordance with the rules governing import duty, however, levying usually precedes the exercise of the right to deduct. Thus, payment takes place within a certain – usually short – period after the date of importation, whereas deduction can be made only after the return period, in which the import took place, has elapsed. The rapid spread of the postponed accounting system in 1969 accordingly caused the Dutch Treasury to record a budgetary shortfall for that year, as a result of the tax arising from importation increasingly being due at the same time as the deduction of this tax was made.

Since payment and deduction are also made on the same return, i.e. that of the entrepreneur for whom the goods are intended, this would appear to be a crafty way of avoiding VAT on imports altogether. It is easily forgotten in the process that the situation as regards internal supplies is essentially no different, although payment and deduction are made on two separate returns. The only budgetary advantage that the United Kingdom and Ireland derive from their recent abolition of the Benelux-type postponed accounting systems that they used to apply, was in fact paid for by the importers or, as the case may be, foreign suppliers who, when the system was abolished, were suddenly required to pay turnover tax earlier than their domestic competitors.[21]

Frequently the objection has been raised that the postponed accounting system is vulnerable to fraud.

Imported goods are usually completely exempt from taxation in the country of export: in VAT countries this is usually done by applying a zero rate.

In this way, the person who manages to avoid postponed accounting on importation and also manages to hide his subsequent transactions from the tax authorities 'earns' the tax on the total value of the goods. He also runs less of a risk that the tax authorities will detect the transaction at his supplier's then he would if he were to buy in the domestic market.

When goods are purchased on the domestic market they are subject to tax, and anybody who wants to keep the (re-)sale of such goods free of tax must also (be able to) keep the purchase off his books; no deduction is claimed therefore, and the levy on the purchase stands. The tax advantage to be gained concerns only the value added, plus possible benefits as regards income tax, etc.

As regards vulnerability of the postponed accounting system to fraud – a sensitive point in countries which do not have such a system – there are various things which can be done. For instance, one can open the scheme only to entrepreneurs who keep books in the manner required by tax law. This is what happens in the Netherlands, except the imports from Belgium and Luxembourg, which are discussed below. In addition, data can be gathered on importation in aid of the tax collection. In the Netherlands this is done by requiring a copy of the invoice.

If the postponed accounting system is used as it should be to achieve the maximum reduction in frontier formalities, the above remedies are less applicable. Thus, since 1971 the postponed accounting system for imports from the Benelux partner countries has applied to all imports by entrepreneurs and bodies within the meaning of the General Revenue Act (Algemene wet inzake rijksbelastingen). Furthermore, the required copy of the invoice was replaced within the Benelux from 1 July 1984 under a special instruction – the Benelux Order 50 (Opgave Benelux 50) – which was brought in to ensure uniform application of the system in the Benelux countries.

---

21. A disadvantage for domestic suppliers is that they are already liable for tax as well on advance payments received; in respect of the importation of goods, such liability is incurred at the earliest at the moment of importation irrespective of any advance payments that have been made.

    As regards the difference in treatment between a subsequent deduction of turnover tax paid on importation and a deduction in respect of domestic supplies preliminary questions have already been referred to the Court of Justice. In its judgment of 10 July 1984, in case 42/83 (Dansk Denkavit) the Court found that such treatment was not in conflict with Article 95 of the EEC Treaty.

XI.5.3.2 Development of the Postponed Accounting System

Frontier formalities can be reduced still further (and possibly replaced entirely) by international cooperation, consisting of the systematic provisions of data, other types of information and assistance. In the Benelux, the Treaty on mutual assistance with regard to the levying of turnover tax, transfer tax and other imports 1964 (subsequently replaced by the more general Benelux Cooperation Agreement 1969) has obviously been used hitherto only in support of administration at the frontier, although in essence it was designed to make it possible to do away with frontier formalities. Similar opportunities for cooperation have been opened up for the Community by the Directive concerning mutual assistance by the competent authorities of the Member States in the field of direct taxation and of value added tax, dating originally from 1977 and amended in 1979 to apply to turnover tax.[22]

The most complete form of cooperation (which also offers the best possibility of doing away with turnover tax formalities for imports within the postponed accounting system) is achieved by systematically linking the application of the zero rate in the country of export to the charging of tax in the country of import. The Benelux 50 Order issued in 1984 was, furthermore, originally designed to do just that, the aim being that a supplier who wished to have the supply of goods exported to a Benelux partner country zero-rated, should make a declaration to that effect.

That declaration could then be used by the relevant partner country to supervise the charging of tax on importation. (For the time being, however, the declaration has to be made at the border.) In 1975, the Benelux countries consulted business circles about this type of system. The declaration was called the 'single administrative document' which initially still had to be produced at the internal border, but once the frontier formalities had been abolished, could be sent direct to a central office.

The idea of linking tax treatment in the countries of export and import was revived in 1981 when Simons drew attention to what he called 'zero-rate notification'.[23] His discussion also included the Clearing House System, which we shall examine in the next section.

At this juncture I shall content myself with the following observation. How important the postponed accounting system may be for business circles, notably as regards financing, and irrespective of the opportunity the system provides – perhaps through international cooperation – of reducing and even doing away with frontier formalities, it must be understood that it still assumes that importation is a taxable event and that on exportation tax is removed (detaxation) by applying a zero-rate or by making a refund (detaxing).

22. Directive 79/1070/EEC implementing Directive 77/799/EEC, O.J. No L 331, 1979.
23. A.L.C. Simons, 'Simplification of VAT Procedures', *op.cit.* note 9 *supra.*

XI.5.4 Clearing House System

The abolition of tax barriers in the Community with a view to establishing one large internal market automatically suggests, as regards turnover taxation, that the importation of goods as a taxable event between Member States on a reciprocal basis must be done away with and that the zero rate on exports to another Member State must be dropped. Of course, the taxable event and the rate will still be significant as regards the movement of goods to and from non-member countries. The resulting situation as regards intra-Community traffic, as suggested in the Clearing House System, is that supplies of goods by traders will be taxed as such, in accordance with the rules in force and at the rate which applies in the Member State of supply, even if the purchaser resides or is established in another Member State and the goods are consequently 'exported' from a Member State of supply. If the purchaser is an entrepreneur, he may also deduct the turnover tax accounted to him by the supplier in the other Member States, and do so in his own Member State.

The system would seem to be perfect, but a few questions do in fact arise. I shall confine myself principally to the extra currency flows generated by payment of VAT. The question is: In what currency shall entrepreneurs account to each other for turnover tax? It would be nice if, by the time a Community VAT system has been established along these lines, there were also a Community currency, which can play a crucial role in this area. If this should not transpire, internationally active entrepreneurs would be faced in the Community with deductible VAT in many currencies which will subsequently have to be converted using different, and possibly also frequently fluctuating, exchange rates into the currency of the country of establishment. The fact is that the Community VAT system is such that the tax to be paid is calculated on the difference between output and input tax, with the result that an entrepreneur established in the Netherlands who resells goods purchased in Germany in the United Kingdom will perhaps have to deduct German marks from pounds to know what he has to pay in guilders. It will also depend considerably on the structure selected for this kind of transaction. Before we go into this further, we shall first examine the role of the different inland revenue departments which deal with the system.

When our entrepreneur, he could accurately be called the 'protagonist', sells the good he bought in Germany to customers in the Netherlands consumption takes place in the Netherlands, but only the tax on the value added there accrues to the Dutch Treasury.[24] The tax 'missed' by the Dutch

---

24. In fact the situation is more complicated. Only if the rates in the Netherlands and Germany were the same, would it be a question of taxing 'the' value added.

   See on this, 'Wertschopfungsland-Prinzip' in D. Biehl, *Ausfuhrlandprinzip, Einfuhrlandprinzip und Gemeinsamer Markt-Prinzip, ein Beitrag zur Theorie der Steuerharmonisierung*, Cologne 1968. *See also* Chapter X.2 *supra*.

tax authorities is in fact the German input tax deducted by the Dutch trader. Under the Clearing House System, however, the Netherlands would claim the German input tax from the German tax authorities. The converse, of course, will also occur, and claims will arise vis-á-vis other Member States. 'Clearing' is the (bilateral) settlement of those claims, hence the name of the system. The system, be it noted too, does not take its name from any positive feature of such an arrangement, but precisely from its most negative one, i.e. the need to offset turnover tax between Member States against tax which, as regards the country of destination principle, has accrued to the wrong treasury.

With the Clearing House System, therefore, we see extra VAT currency flows from entrepreneur to entrepreneur in commerce between the Member States and the accompanying payments by suppliers to the authorities and correspondingly claims for deduction from customers. Subsequently, the Member States then settle payments and deductions on a reciprocal basis (*see also* Chapter XII.4.1 *infra*).

The above arrangement entails complications

    a. for entrepreneurs, who pay their contributions in other Member States and have to offset VAT accounted for in a foreign country against their own VAT and

    b. for the tax authorities in the Member States who then have to clear the amounts in question between them.

The question arises whether those authorities will not be tempted as regards the reciprocal settlements to place (extra) administrative obligations on their traders, such as the separate administration and declaration (including differences in the rate of tax) of the input tax accruing to the different Member States. Finally, it is not impossible that Member States will require each other to submit accurate and very specifc VAT claims, with the right of inspection as regards both the Member States concerned and, possibly, the entrepreneurs established in the State being invested either in themselves or a Community body.

XI.5.5 A Clearing System Without Clearing

While it is self-evident that the Clearing House System does indeed do away with frontier problems, – i.e. it is no longer necessary, at any rate, to relieve the tax burden on exports and charge tax on imports – other and, in my opinion, serious complications arise.[25] It seems to me that under the Clearing

---

25. Zero-rate notification (*see* XI.5) may solve many of the complications as regards the extra monetary flows. There is also the question, however, of the (legal) basis for such zero-rating. If the intention is, within a single internal market to abandon the concept of exportation, and

House System the levy and, hence, deduction occur at the wrong place. This question of where supplies are charged, or if one wishes, the place of supply, is a fundamental one.

The Community Directive (that is, the Sixth Directive) at present reckons that place in principle to be where the importation associated with the supply begins or, as the case may be, where the goods are at the time of supply (see Article 8(1) of the Sixth Directive). This suggests that, in respect of goods transported from one country to another, the place of supply should not be in the State of departure, but *in the purchaser's country*.[26] The charge will then usually be imposed in the same country as that where the (subsequent) deduction is claimed.

This automatically obviates many of the problems outlined above such as currency differences and settlement between Member States. At first sight, the disadvantage of this proposal is that the Member States must include the foreign suppliers concerned in their national collection of VAT. The Sixth Directive, however, has a solution for this, namely to charge the purchaser, the so-called deferred payment (*see* the second sentence of Article 21(1) of the Sixth Directive.)[27] Charging the purchaser means in effect that the 'clearing' component in the Clearing House System no longer applies.

At first sight, there is hardly a difference to the postponed accounting system for imports discussed in 5.3.2 *supra*. Instead of the importation being the event, the purchaser is now charged tax on the supply of goods which, however, have still been 'imported', and the zero rate is replaced by the non-taxation of the supplier (in this case in respect of goods supplied which have left the country).

For all the thinking behind the Clearing House System really to produce results, however, we no longer need to worry about where the goods are

---

the zero-rate based thereon, there should be no question, in my opinion, of granting certain entrepreneurs relief of tax (in order, notably, to negate the risk of non-payment) merely because they are established in another Member State, when such a facility is not available domestically.

26. What is advocated in fact is the 'purchase principle' as it applies to a considerable extent to the place where a service is supplied (*see* note 19 above). The transport-based approach is thus expressly disregarded. In conformity with the place of service, the place of delivery for immovable properties is the locus situs; the delivery will be taxed according to rates of the country of location.

27. In the Netherlands, this method of charging VAT was retained by the legislator from earlier turnover tax legislation. Under this, the purchaser was acknowledged initially to be jointly liable, as is still the case at present in most of the other Member States. As regards transactions with foreign purchasers, liability was not subject to any limit. As a result, it often happened that domestic purchasers paid turnover tax twice, i.e. firstly in the price to their foreign supplier or provider of services and secondly to the Dutch tax authorities. At the instigation of Dutch business circles, this system was replaced in 1965 by charging the domestic purchaser (Article 18(2) of the Turnover Tax Act 1965).

supplied, as long as that place is within the territory of the Community. If we regard the internal market as a single whole, as the respective territories are now, then it must be immaterial whether the goods which, for instance, are supplied by a German trader to a Dutch customer are already in the Netherlands, carried there from Germany or another Member State, or perhaps do not enter the Netherlands at all but stay in Germany, Belgium or France or are perhaps even transported to the latter countries instead of to the Netherlands. When VAT is charged in, say, the Netherlands, on the supply by a trader established in Rotterdam to a customer in Amsterdam, it is unimportant whether the goods are in Rotterdam or Leeuwarden, or whether they are perhaps in transit to Amsterdam or Groningen.

There are in fact two options: the supply is taxed either at the supplier stage (in that person's Member State), or at the purchaser stage (in that person's Member State).

In the former case, we are again faced with the disadvantages described above of the Clearing House System. If tax is imposed in the purchaser's country, then obviously – as already argued – the levy too, must also be at the purchaser. Once again, this is the Clearing House System without the 'clearing' component, with the great advantage that the actual movements of goods within the territory of the Community no longer matter and therefore no longer need to be administered and monitored, no more than when this occurs within one Member State. As the Community system of VAT also covers retailing, such an arrangement hardly seems to be a problem: in principle, the consumer buys in shops in countries where he is resident. Only passenger traffic is a problem and it is discussed in more detail in Section 5.7 *infra*.

Where purchases are made by exempt entrepreneurs, by bodies which are not entrepreneur or by authorities, taxation can also be carried out in the country of the purchaser, whereby payment can be deferred to the purchaser, as is already provided for in the Netherlands in Article 12(2) of the turnover Tax Act 1968.[28]

As well as passenger traffic, there are other cases where goods are supplied to individuals in another Member State, i.e. by mail order companies.

Here too, it seems to me that the direct taxation of, say, the mail order company by the country where the customer(s) is (are) resident is better than deferment to the customer. A Community solution, to be applied by the

28. The exempt use in one Member State of goods which were purchased by the buyer concerned in another Member State for use that is subject to tax, and *vice versa*, could be a problem. The present solution – adjustment of the prior deduction – seems to have a less favorable effect in the other Member State (*see* Article 15(3) of the Turnover Tax Act 1968 and the implementing provisions based thereon, and Article 20 of the Sixth Directive). In such cases, however, a 'self-supply' charge such as that levied in respect of own manufacturers (*see* Article 3(1) (h) of the Turnover Tax Act 1968), as discussed in Section 5.2 could provide a solution.

Member State in which the mail order company is established, is by no means inconceivable.

Finally, the remarks in Section 5.3 with regard to the application of the Directive on mutual assistance and a possible system of notification based on the supplier's books (which I will term *'diversion notification'*) also apply of course to the clearing system without the 'clearing' component discussed here.

XI.5.6 Approximation of VAT Rates

Among all the possible ways discussed above of reducing or abolishing frontier formalities in commercial traffic, no mention has been made of the rates applied in the different Member States. It is, of course, possible to argue that rate levels are irrelevant. This may be justified in theory, but in practice, where the scope for fraud is concerned, rates are definitely significant. A simple example may suffice. A Dutch florist sells flowers to a Belgian fellow trader who sells them in his own country to individuals. In theory, the Dutchman will claim zero-rating (or some other relief from Dutch tax incurred previously).

In Belgium, 19% VAT is then charged (the current rate in Belgium). With the 'link' with Belgium, not taken into account, however, the Dutchman has to pay only 6% VAT, whereas the turnover in Belgium is kept hidden from the tax authorities.

The objection could be made that, in the foregoing, we have only referred – and wrongly – to the arrangements discussed, in which the supplier in fact remains untaxed. With the 'genuine' Clearing House System, however, this is not the case since the supplier does charge VAT to the customer. Yet this does not produce a different situation to that already described. In Section 5.3.3 we discussed *inter alia* the susceptibility of the postponed accounting system to fraud in a domestic taxation context. What we said was that fraud usually implies that purchases are not entered in the books; domestically – at any rate as regards VAT – only the tax on the value added is thus 'earned' as opposed to the whole VAT in the case of fraudulent imports. In the above example, where an arrangement applies which in a way short-circuits the tax situation of supplier and customer, the difference in rate between Belgium and the Netherlands is also 'earned'. This is also the case, however, under the Commission's Clearing House System.

If, under that system, the Belgian trader leaves the purchase which he made in the Netherlands off his books then he 'earns' not only the Belgian 19% on his value added but also the difference between the Belgian input tax at 19% and the Dutch input tax at 6%.

The Commission is in my opinion correct in assuming that within given limits certain differences are acceptable. Taking trade alone, the question really is what difference will be enough to make fraud unattractive. If we look at the various rates currently applied in the Community, it is clear that both standard and reduced rates vary within certain 'bands'.[29] There are relatively large differences between standard and reduced rates and, in the countries where increased rates are applied, between the standard rate and the increased rates.

In view of the debate about a uniform VAT rate in the Netherlands, I wonder whether it is really sensible to explore the possibility of applying a uniform rate in all Member States (whether or not with permitted fluctuations within a given band).

The reasons which underlie the Dutch two-rate system and which obviously make that system difficult to give up will most probably have their counterparts in the other Member States.

In view of the foregoing, the conclusion that a two-rate system within a given band is the maximum that can be achieved is inescapable. Agreement will simply have to be reached about which goods may or may not be subject to a reduced rate. (*See further* Chapter XII.3.1 *infra*.) In my opinion it is not necessary to make this compulsory: a Member State which wishes within its own borders to apply a standard rate to goods which are elsewhere taxed at the reduced rate is taking the attendant risk itself. The same applies to the maintenance of existing rates or the introduction of new, higher ones.

XI.5.7 The Individual Traveler

Following the above, I can be brief on the individual traveler. Anyone wishing to leave travel really free – at any rate as regards VAT, excises may perhaps be different – will accept the country of origin principle. If one wants to avoid individuals crossing borders en masse in order to shop, it is also necessary to approximate rates, as discussed under Section 4.4. Complete harmonization, in my opinion, is not necessary for travel either.

I noted earlier that the problems of cross-border purchases of goods by individuals are not just confined to travel. In particular, there are the mail order firms operating internationally (*see also* 5.5 above). As regards the occasional sending of goods purchased from retailers in another Member State, or the ordering of such goods by individuals, the same philosophy could perhaps apply as in the case of travel.

---

29. It is noteworthy that the Commission is proposing a band of 5 per cent (2.5 per cent on either side of the standard rate or rates). In practice, most Member States appear to operate to all intents and purposes in whole percentage points. A 4 per cent or 6 per cent band would be more appropriate.

There is, moreover, still a wide range of cases between 'genuine' mail order firms and dealers who may or may not occasionally send goods to individuals in other countries. It may, therefore, become necessary – with a view both to preventing deflection of trade and allocating tax revenue to the Member States correctly – to apply a possible 'mail order firm arrangement' to a much larger category of traders than mail order firms proper.

XI.5.8 Excises and Special Taxes on Consumption

As has already been pointed out (in Section 5.2), the problems of excises and (other) special taxes on consumption in a single internal market are fundamentally different from those associated with taxes such as VAT.[30] This is the result of the difference in the charging system: in principle, excises are levied at the manufacturing stage, i.e. far from the consumer, while VAT is levied up to and including the retail stage, i.e. very close to the consumer.

The pattern of excise duties and special taxes on consumption is already so complex in one country, e.g. the Netherlands, that discussion of what can be done to help complete the internal market and remove frontier formalities is hardly possible in a few paragraphs. I would like to make a few comments nevertheless.

Apart from the system of levying, excises and special taxes on consumption also differ from a general tax on consumption such as VAT in that they are levied on a limited number of categories of goods. Most of these goods are of a special nature.

Without going into more detail, it must be said that in the case of some of the categories of goods concerned, supervision or registration may be such – sometimes for reasons which have nothing to do with the collection of tax – that solutions to the frontier problems are possible. One example of such a registration system is provided in the Netherlands by the special tax on motor cars and motorcycles. Stamp systems such as that used for the excise duty on tobacco or that which is occasionally advocated with regard to distiller's excise duty also offer possible solutions. For the rest, it should be realized that frontier checks would then in fact be replaced by domestic ones on number plates, the stamps used, and so on. On the other hand, however, such checks already exist for the most part, either independently (as with the registration of number plates) or for reasons to do with domestic taxation (tobacco stamps).

30. It is noteworthy that the White Paper refers to the 'striking example' of the United States in connection with turnover tax only. In the US, excises are also regulated autonomously by the States themselves and caused restrictions in the inter-State carriage of goods. The differences in charging have not led, however, to harmonization or other measures designed to create a single market for the goods in question.

It may also occur that the collection of an excise duty is not only linked to production and importation, but that the commercial stage also plays a role.

As long as the taxation is not final and the goods in question are accordingly subject to a degree of supervision, arrangements similar to those applying in the case of VAT are conceivable. In principle, when goods are transferred from one bonded warehouse to another, it is immaterial whether a border is crossed or not. However, there is the difficulty in such a case that systems involving bonded warehouses, or other arrangements whereby excise is deferred, are usually voluntary. Only if, with regards to a particular excise duty for example, the entire wholesale trade were made subject to a supervisory system could such systems offer certain possibilities.

If the circumstances outlined above provide no way out, there is in my opinion only one solution: uniform Community excises, with the yield allocated to the Member States on the basis of macrodata concerning national consumption of the dutiable goods concerned. This was also the solution envisaged in the Benelux, but even after the conclusion of the Benelux Treaty on the unification of excise duties and customs deposit law in 1950, no further progress has been made beyond the harmonization of the excise duty on wine that had already been introduced in 1948. That, as a result of such harmonization, the excise duty on wine is still relatively low compared with excise duties in respect of which such harmonization has not as yet been achieved, e.g. the excise duty on beer or the distiller's excise duty, was probably not the intention, but it has been welcomed by wine lovers. The attraction of this approach is not just that both trade and travel can be liberalized completely, but that basically the country of destination principle can also be complied with.

XI.5.9 Sketch of a Complete System

As we have seen, a non cumulative tax on consumption that includes the retail stage allows for several ways of simplification or even abolishment of border procedures.

When we consider a group of countries like the Member States of the European Community, we have to take into account that we are confronted with two kinds of borders within the Community between Member States.

It has been argued that within the Community with regard to transactions between entrepreneurs, the tax should be levied in the country of the purchaser, regardless of where in the territory of the Member States the goods are stored or moving. Because the tax is levied in this way up to the retail stage and the retailer is taxed in his own country for delivering goods to the consumers who buy their good in that country, there is no infringement of the country of destination principle except in the case of the individual traveler who buys his goods in another country of the Community.

The question must be raised if such a system can also be used in cases where goods are imported into or exported from the Community. In my view, two conditions have to be met for the proposed system to be feasible: there has to be a system of notification based on the supplier's books and there has to be an approximation of rates. Both conditions are not easy to bring about in relation with countries outside the Community.

Therefore in my opinion for imports in the Community a postponed accounting system along the lines of the proposed 14th Directive is advisable, provided the taxation is postponed to the purchaser of the goods, regardless of the destination of the goods within the Community. Customs officers can collect on importation the information that otherwise within the Community is derived from the supplier's books. Once the goods are within the Community the above-mentioned system is applicable.

On exportation from the Community, tax has to be removed by applying a zero rate (detaxation). A special case arises if the supplier or purchaser of goods that are already within the Community is established outside the Community. If the seller is established outside the Community it may seem that taxation of the purchaser can be endangered because no information is obtained either on importation or from the supplier's books. However, in these cases the supplier or an earlier supplier must have imported the goods, or the goods must have been bought from an earlier supplier who is established in the Community.[31]

Finally, the foreign entrepreneur from a third country needs to be considered as a domestic taxable person only in one Member State to be included in the system, which covers the trade with third countries by postponed accounting and the trade between Member States by deferred payment.

XI.5.10 Some Examples

In my view, every proposal to abolish or simplify border procedures should be tested with a few practical cases in mind, with the purposes of measuring their effectiveness their completeness, and eventually their flaws. I even think one test case is sufficient.

A, established in country W, supplies goods that at that moment stored in country X to a purchaser B, established in country Y, who wants the goods to be delivered somewhere in country Z. In turn A and B and their respective countries can be considered to be within or outside the Community; likewise

---

31. Likewise a purchaser who is not established within the Community is charged with tax upon importation unless he is established in one of the Member States as a taxable person, in which case he can be included in the postponed accounting system. Furthermore, because an entrepreneur sells *and* buys goods, it will be to his advantage to be included in the system anyway.

countries X and Z can in turn be considered to be Member States or third countries.

The questions to be asked are the following:

1. Is importation the taxable event, or the delivery of the goods?
2. Is A the taxable person or B?
3. In which country does A or B have to pay the tax?
4. Surely B is entitled to deduction of that tax, but in which country can he exercise this right?
5. Does A or B have to pay tax according to foreign rates and in foreign currency?
6. Is the tax that B is entitled to deduct in foreign currency?
7. Which country has to compensate which other country?

While answering these questions, it should also be taken into consideration that both A and B are international traders, who are doing business with more countries inside and outside the Community. It is easy to be seen that in the proposed clearing system without clearing (*see* XI.5.5) it is always B that has to pay the tax, whether it is on importation if the goods are imported from country X outside the Community, or on account of the purchasing if the goods are not imported into the Community (i.e. country X is inside the Community).

The tax is always to be paid in the country where B is established, against the rates and in the currency of that same country. If B sells the goods to a person who is established in that same country, B has the right of deduction of the same domestic tax against his obligation to pay tax on the subsequent delivery; the same holds true if the purchaser is established in another Member State and the deferred payment system diverts the taxation to that person; do the goods travel to a country Z outside the Community than a zero is applicable. In the case that the goods are sold within the Community to a person; do the goods travel to a country Z outside the Community then the zero rate is applicable. In the case that the goods are sold within the Community to a person who is not established in any of the Member States, the delivery in my view should be taxed, with the aim of not losing control of the designed taxation of goods that are not exported from the Community.

Chapter XII. The Creation of an Internal Market; Follow up to the White Paper

XII.1 INTRODUCTION

In the summer of 1987 the Commission of the European Community issued a global communication,[1] a working document[2] and proposals for seven directives[3] presenting a blueprint of the fiscal aspects of completion of the internal market.[4] The Commission's proposals are largely based on the strategy provided for in the White Paper (*see* Chapter XI *supra*). Two aspects however, the VAT-clearing and the approximation of the excises, depart from the White Paper.

The Commission ascertains that its blueprint provides the detailed proposals for which the European Council of Ministers for Financial Affairs (ECOFIN) have asked. In June 1986[5] the ECOFIN reserved its position until

1. Completion of the internal market: approximation of indirect tax rates and harmonization of indirect tax structure. Global communication from the Commission. Com (87) 320 final.
2. Completing the internal market – the introduction of a VAT clearing mechanism for intra-community sales. Working document from the Commission. Com (87) 323 final.
3. Proposal for a Council Directive completing the common system of value added tax and amending Directive 77/388/EEC – Approximation of VAT rates – Com (87) 321 final; Proposal for a Council Directive completing and amending Directive 77/388/EEC – Removal of fiscal frontiers – Com (87) 322 final; Proposal for a Council Directive instituting a process of convergence of rates of value-added tax and excise duties Com (87) 324 final (replacing the 'standstill' proposal, *see* Chapter XI, note 14.); and four proposals on the approximation of cigarette taxes, of manufactured tobacco other than cigarettes, of excise duties on mineral oils and of excise duties on alcoholic beverages and other products containing alcohol, Com (87) 325 through 328.
4. The European Single Act, amending the EEC-Treaty, (O.J. 1987, L 169) establishes as a legal commitment the objective of an *internal market* to be reached by the end of 1992. The (new) article 8A of the EEC-Treaty describes the internal market as 'an area without frontiers in which the free movement of goods, persons, services and capital is ensured'.
5. Previously (in Milan, June 1985) the European Council invited the ECOFIN to examine on the basis of the White Paper any measures which might be necessary for the achievement of a single market and the possible timetable for the application of those measures. The ECOFIN delegated this mandate at first instance to a high level group of fiscal experts, who concluded that Member States will not be able to decide whether the measures envisaged by the

the Commission had submitted to the Council 'detailed proposals on the rates and rate structure of indirect taxation and on the clearing system'.

The present proposals are the basis on which the Member States will be in a position to weigh up the implications for themselves, and to determine what benefits and what costs they offer to each of them in their own particular circumstances, both in the shorter and the longer term. Eventual adjustments are possible, the Commission is even prepared to examine with the Member States concerned what special measures might be applied to them. Provided are possible, the Commission is even prepared to examine with the Member States concerned what special measures might be applied to them, provided such measures are of a temporary nature and cause the least possible distur- The proposals allow a degree of flexibility and a reasonable time of adjustment; the proposals should enter into force *no later than 31 December 1992*. It will be the responsibility of the individual Member States to work towards the envisaged adjustments.

XII.2 THE PROPOSALS

The White Paper demonstrated that in order to abolish fiscal frontiers there must be a considerable measure of approximation of indirect taxes.[6] In its global communication the Commission proposes four major changes in the present system of indirect taxation within the Community.[7]

First, the Commission proposes an approximation of the VAT and the main excise duties.[8] Only two VAT rates will be allowed, a standard rate, within a range of seven points, of 14 to 20 per cent and a reduced rate of 5 to 9 per cent. Regarding the excise duties, as early as 1972 the Commission singled out for retention and harmonization at Community level the excises on manufactured tobacco, mineral oils, spirits, wine and beer. Now, common rates of excise duties are proposed on harmonized structures.

Second, the Commission proposes to eliminate the distinction made at

---

Commission are ultimately acceptable to them until full details of the measures as a whole are available.

6. In the previous chapter I concluded that approximation of rates is necessary even in the presented alternative system of abolishment of fiscal frontiers: the clearing system without clearing.

7. The proposals are restricted to VAT and excises. There are, of course, other indirect taxes within the Community, such as taxes on registration of vehicles, and on the purchases of houses which vary considerably from Member State to Member State. Although these variations can be as such causes to distortions of competition and deflection of trade, they do not impede the free movement of goods in the sense that they cause fiscal frontiers.

8. It should be noted here that the Commission (finally) proposes harmonization of indirect taxes *in their relation to – each other* as emphasized in the Deringer-report 24-years earlier (*see* note 15, Chapter VIII *supra*).

present between supplies within a Member State and supplies to another Member State. For intra-Community trade the existing system of relieving goods from tax at export and of imposing tax at import will be abolished.

Third, a (revised) VAT clearing mechanism is proposed, to ensure the destination principle between the Member States. In essence the mechanism is a central account through which Member States will draw or pay money periodically, depending on the extent to which they are net importers or net exporters.[9]

Fourth, the Commission proposes (for VAT purposes) to change the place of taxable transactions regarding the services. The Commission proposes to amend the Sixth Directive in order to treat services in the same ways as sales and purchase of goods. We will deal with these proposals in the following sections.

XII.3 Approximation of VAT and Excise Duties

For ease of analysis, VAT and excise duties are dealt with separately.

XII.3.1 VAT

Although considerable progress has been made towards the creation of a common VAT base,[10] notably with the adoption of the Sixth Directive (*see* Chapter VIII *supra*), further measures are necessary to abolish fiscal frontiers. The proposals of the Commission on approximation of VAT rates and the rate structure are related to 1. the number of rates, 2. the coverage of the distinct rates, and 3. the rate levels.

Regarding the *number of rates* the Commission refers to the existing situation in the Member States. Ten out of twelve Member States apply more than one rate.[11] Although, in theory, a VAT system with only one rate is the simplest and most efficient structure, it is clear that such an approach would have disruptive consequences for all, but two, Member States and is unlikely

---

9. For excise duties no such system is needed, since these are not charged until the goods are released from bond. Normally in the country in which they are to be sold to the final consumer.
10. Additionally, the Commission has put forward several proposals, notably the Twelfth, Eighteenth and Nineteenth draft Directives (*see* Chapter VIII.7 *supra*) designed to eliminate some of the most significant areas of divergence. The Commission urges the Council to deal with these proposals as a matter of urgency. The Seventh, Fourteenth and Sixteenth draft Directives are withdrawn.
11. Only Denmark and the UK apply one rate, the UK however applies the zero-rate extensively.

to be acceptable as a whole.[12] The choice is between a three rate (reduced, standard and increased) and a two rate (reduced, standard) system. Clearly, a three rate system creates (even) more complications for both national administrations and taxpayers. The existing increased rates in the Member States applying them, differ widely and furthermore their abolition will not create undue financial problems since they are only applied to a relatively small proportion of the tax base. For these reasons the Commissions prefers a two rate system.

Regarding the *coverage of the rates*, the reduced rate should, in conformity with the present practices in the Community, apply to items of basic necessity; mainly foodstuffs with the exception of alcoholic drinks, energy products for heating and lighting, supplies of water, pharmaceutical products, books, newpapers and periodicals and passenger transport.[13]

The Commission deems it necessary to narrow the *differences in the spread of rates* between certain limits, in order to avoid intolerable tax induced price-differences between (especially adjacent) Member States.[14] For the standard rate the Commission proposes a permitted range of between 14 and 20 per cent, (Under these parameters 7 Member States would currently fall within this range),[15] for the reduced rate[16] a range between 4 and 9 per cent.

XII.3.2 Excises

The approximation of the excise duties is basically a processs of unification. Based on its proposals of 1972 the Commission singles out for retention and

12. The Commission's approach is remarkably pragmatic, based on what is (politically) most feasible. The Commission has refrained from proposing anything which is not strictly necessary for the purpose of the implementation of article 99 of the EEC-Treaty. this might very well be the Achilles' Heel of the proposals. Major fiscal changes in one field of taxation (i.e. the indirect taxes) hardly come alone, they inhere in pressures on the other field (i.e. the direct taxes). This may place additional strains on Member States, which may be politically (relating to the fiscal sovereignty) unacceptable. *See also* note 18 *infra*.
13. Overall these items represent approximately one-third of the common Community tax base.
14. Separately the Commission deals with the problem of zero rates and other derogations and exemptions. The Commission explains that it has always been an accepted part of Community policy that zero-rating except in the case of exports, is a temporary measure which would disappear with the completion of the internal market.
15. Again (*cf.* note 12 *supra*) this is a rather pragmatic approach. The question arises however how this permitted range of seven points relates to the range of 5 points mentioned in the White Paper, based on 'experience' in the USA. In addition to this there are serious reasons to believe that rate differences even of 5 per cent do cause major intolerable (tax-induced) price differences, a diversion of trade and tax-fraud in the USA (for example between Massachusetts and New Hampshire.) Between adjacent Member States therefore it is to be expected that a process of *enforced* harmonization will take place.
16. The Commission recommends that Member States fix their rate in the lower half of that band!

unification at Community level the excises on manufactured tobacco, mineral oils, spirits, wine and beer. The Commission proposes amounts in ECU for all specific duties and percentages for the ad valorem duties on manufactured tobaccoes thus leaving some extra flexibility in these rates of duties. For all excised commodities some flexibility is permitted by the VAT rates, resulting in possible tax-induced price differentials well in excess of 5%.

In order to prevent any further increase in the existing differences between national systems of indirect taxation, the Commission proposes[17] the prohibition of any divergence in the number or level of VAT rates at present applied by the Member States, while at the same time allowing and indeed encouraging, convergence towards the number and level of VAT rates.

Similarly, for the above mentioned excises only changes which converge towards the rates of duty proposed by the Commission would be allowed. The introduction of new excise duties, which give rise to control at internal frontiers would be prohibited.[18]

XII.4 REMOVAL OF FISCAL FRONTIERS – A VAT CLEARING MECHANISM

In its working document the Commission proposes a *revised clearing mechanism*, that departs from the clearing system envisaged in the White Paper.

XII.4.1 Background

The clearing system, as proposed in the White Paper, was discussed in the Council ad hoc fiscal group (*see* note 5 *supra*). In essence this system was based on bilateral clearing between the Member States (*see* Chapter XI *supra*) using aggregated input tax figures submitted by the taxable person. Transfers between the Member States would be expressed in ECU. At a certain period, perhaps once a year, there would be a reconciliation between Member States claims. The *ad hoc* group concluded that checks and controls needed to be reconsidered in order to provide a sound basis for the substantial revenue involved.

Following this the Commission examined the possibility of using listing

---

17. In a new draft Directive Com (87) 324 final *see* note 3 *supra*.
18. It is questionable whether all Member States are willing to accept the budgetary effects of the proposals. It seems probable that for three Member States (Belgium, Italy and the Netherlands) the proposals are budgetary neutral, France would suffer a slight budgetary loss, three Member States (Germany, UK and Greece) would obtain small or moderate increases in budgetary receipts, Ireland and Denmark however would suffer pronounced budgetary losses. Luxembourg, Spain and Portugal would obtain substantial increases in budgetary receipts (*see also* note 12 *supra*).

systems, establishing exact pictures of individual traders' activities. The listing system could provide a basis for matching input tax against output tax for individual traders without descending to the level of bringing individual invoices to account. The Commission feared that notwithstanding the necessary considerable administrative efforts, it would be highly improbable that a reasonable level of matching between the different lists could be obtained.

Against this background the Commission designed an alternative proposal[19] based on the following criteria:

1. The primary objective is the creation of a soundly based and reliable system to attribute to the appropriate Member State[20] VAT collected on intra community sales.
2. The additional burden on traders must be kept to a minimum.
3. The clearing mechanism should fit into the existing VAT administrative structure of Member States with the minimum of disruption, thus grafted onto existing national tax collection systems, based on self-assessed periodical declarations of the tax payable.
4. The system should be based on the matching of individual transactions.[21]
5. The clearing system should be self-financing. In the Commission's proposal two separate but interlinked problems are dealt with: the clearing system itself and a system of controls and checks. These subjects will be dealt with separately.

XII.4.2 The Clearing Mechanism

The Commission has come to the conclusion that the clearing system does *not* need to operate on the basis of bilateral flows between Member States and that it can operate simply on the basis of money owed to or from a *central account*. Into this account – serviced by the Commission and operated exclusively in terms of the ECU – net importing countries will be required to pay and net exporting countries will receive payments from the account. Under the proposed system Member States will provide a monthly statement indicating its total VAT input and output figures for intra-Community trade (without being dependent on bilateral clearing or on a yearly balancing of VAT accounts). These monthly payments by the Member States, and consequential payments to and from the clearing account, are part of a perpetually

---

19. According to article 4 of the proposal regarding the removal of fiscal frontiers – Com (87) 322 final – the proposals of the Commission regarding the clearing mechanism will have to be adopted in an appropriate *regulation*.
20. Based on the destination principle.
21. A system based on a purely macro-economic approach is unlikely to provide an acceptable level of accuracy.

on-going process – never representing a fiscal balancing of the VAT-accounts.

There will be no need for traders to include separate input tax figures for purchases in each Member State, they simply will have to fill in two extra boxes on their normal declaration indicating the output and input VAT on intra-Community trade as a whole. Each Member State will aggregate and convert the information received on traders' declarations into ECU before transmitting its monthly statement to the Commission's Services. A noteworthy feature of the system is that the clearing account will show a *surplus* approximately equal to the VAT charged on intra-Community sales to VAT-exempt businesses and other entities (as well as to private persons).[22] It is intended that this surplus will be distributed periodically to the Member States.

The Commission considers that the revised system[23] has the following important benefits:

1. Each Member State is reponsible for determining its own net position *vis-à-vis* the clearing account.
2. Minimal additional administrative requirements are imposed on traders.
3. No compensating payments (prior till a final settlement) are necessary on account to net creditor countries.
4. No annual reconciliation is required.
5. The system is entirely self-funding.
6. The system will allow reallocation of a surplus to Member States.

XII.4.3 Controls and Checks

Basically the clearing system could operate without any controls other than simple audit checks, but large flows of revenue are at stake and the opening up of the internal market necessitates close co-operation between the administrations of the Member States to avoid fraud or simple errors. A control system must be credible while not imposing heavy new tasks on traders or administrations. Nevertheless some enhancement of controls should be acceptable to both traders and administrations given the benefits they will derive from the abolition of fiscal frontiers. However, the control procedures

---

22. It should be noted that all retail sales will be excluded from the clearing operation, but that on the other hand mail-order sales between Member States will be included. In my view the Commission overlooks the possibilities offered by article 5 (7) (a) of the Sixth Directive, based on which an 'integration levy' is also possible for *purchases* by VAT-exempt businesses. Uniform application in the Community would result in a much lower surplus than anticipated.
23. In contrast with the previously envisaged bilateral system. One may refer to the revised system as the multilateral clearing system.

for intra-Community trade should be based on the same principles applied to domestic VAT, which are largely based on the self policing nature of the system. In addition to this the ending of zero rating for intra-Community 'exports' will eliminate one of the main areas of potential fraud that exists at present in the country of export.

The Commission proposes coordinated control measures including the following elements: clearly defined audit requirements, intensified administrative cooperation between the Member States, greater use of agreed sampling techniques and credibility checks in respect of cross-frontier trade and a degree of central coordination. Details of these measures have to be developed.[24]

XII.5 SERVICES

From the outset of VAT in the Community, services were not accompanied by border tax adjustments. The place of the taxable transaction is, according to the Sixth Directive, generally the place where the supplier of a service has a fixed establishment from which the service is supplied.[25] The Commission proposes to amend the Sixth Directive in order to treat intra-Community services similar to the supply of goods.[26] The removal of fiscal frontiers makes it unnecessary to continue to link the supply of services listed in Article 6(2) (e) of the Sixth Directive to the customer's country (within the Community). Under the proposed clearing system tax charged in the supplier's country will be deductible in the customer's country.

In the light of the Commission's proposals this makes sense. Still it is remarkable that the system used for services, that has proven to be efficient (especially by using the deferred payment system) has not been taken as starting-point for the delivery of goods. Of course the result would have been the clearing system without clearing (*see* Chapter XI *supra*). Be it as it is, the place of services follows the place of supplies of goods.[27] It should be

24. In the working document the initial elements are further considered under four headings:
   1. checks built into the clearing mechanism itself (self policing nature, changes in surplus);
   2. standardized audit trails and information requirements (e.g. adoption of the 'best' practices);
   3. improved control and co-operation at the level of national administrations (e.g. bilateral checking);
   4. improved control co-operation and coordination (centralized Community supervision).
25. Or in absence of such a place of business or fixed establishment, the place where he has his permanent address or usually resides. *See* about the place of services Chapter VIII and IX *supra*.
26. Com (87) 322 final *see* note 3 *supra*.
27. Also the territorial application with regard to transportation has been reformulated, anticipating a proposal for a separate directive dealing with passenger transport, the fiscal charge is linked to the country of departure.

remembered that in the Commission's proposals the importation of goods does not create a taxable event (anymore). In intra-Community trade import and export (of goods and services) will have lost their meaning for indirect taxation.

XII.6 CONCLUSION

The Commission's proposals for a Europe without (fiscal) frontiers are bold and radical. I expect that many alterations will be suggested. Eventually choices will have to be made, the final choice is between progress or decline. On this the White Paper did not mince its words: 'Europe stands at the cross-roads. We either go ahead – with resolution and determination – or we drop back into mediocrity. We can now either resolve to complete the integration of the economies of Europe; or through a lack of political will to face the immense problems involved, we can simply allow Europe to develop into no more than a free trade area.

The difference is crucial. A well-developed free trade area offers significant advantages: it is something much better than that which exists today. But it would fail and fail dismally to release the energies of the people of Europe; it would fail to deploy Europe's immense resources to the maximum advantage; and it would fail to satisfy the aspirations of the people of Europe.'

Chapter XIII. The Superiority of VAT

XIII.1 INTRODUCTION

The foregoing chapters on tax frontiers may incline unsuspecting readers to favor retail sales taxation, or even an(y) other form of a sales tax above VAT. Indeed, in spite of VAT's wide-spread adoption, it is far from universally agreed that VAT is the best solution to taxing consumption.[1] Comparing the various systems of levying a sales tax, (*see* Chapters IV and V *supra*) it seems to me that VAT has only one serious competitor: the retail sales tax (RST). In fact there is broad agreement among lawyers, tax administrators and economists that the only acceptable techniques of levying a sales tax are VAT and RST.[2]

As mentioned earlier (*see* Chapter VI.4.6), a VAT that includes the retail stage is conceptually not different from a single levy at the retail stage. Thus the question is legitimate, whether a VAT should be preferred or a RST?

In this final chapter, the VAT will be evaluated against RST using some of the topics that have been dealt with in the first part of this book, namely the neutrality and the legal character, (Chapters II and III), elements derived from the techniques of levying (Chapters IV and V) and the phenomenon of exemptions (Chapter VI.4).

It is my belief that VAT offers most advantages of an efficient sales tax.

XIII.2 NEUTRALITY AND LEGAL CHARACTER

Bearing in mind that 'there is no such thing as a truly neutral tax system,'[3] the criterion of *neutrality* in sales taxation encounters two distinct, but inter-

---

1. VAT is used by 17 of the 24 members of the Organization for Economic Cooperation and Development (OECD), of the other seven Iceland and Switzerland do apply a retail sales tax, as do most of the US states and all Canadian provinces except one. S. Cnossen, 'VAT and RST: A Comparison', *Canadian Tax Journal* 1987, p. 567.
2. *Idem* p. 574.
3. A.J. Easson, 'Fiscal Discrimination: New Perspectives on Article 95 of the EEC Treaty', C.M.L. Rev. 1981, p. 521.

linked, (main) causes of distortion: 1. the (limited) *coverage* of the tax and 2. the treatment of *import, and exports* (both at an international and an inter-state or intra-Community level).

Regarding the *legal character* it can be argued that the criterion of neutrality and the legal character, that of a 'general indirect tax on consumption', both, each from its different (economic or legal) angle generate the same results. Clearly the concepts are not identical. Whatever is economically feasible is not therefore legal (or enforceable) and vice-versa. Still the major subjects in sales taxation that may contravene the legal character correspond with the two previously mentioned problems regarding neutrality. In the next subsections the differences between VAT and RST regarding these problems will be examined.

XIII.2.1 Coverage of the Tax

Both the 'general' character and the internal neutrality require that a sales tax is a broad based tax. Notwithstanding the many similarities[4] between the RST and VAT, it is precisely the (more) limited[5] coverage of services in a retail sales tax, that makes this form of taxation less attractive both from a neutrality point of view, and as viewed from the 'general' character. The question arises why governments excluded (most) services when setting up a retail sales tax. Generally this is caused by the administrative difficulty of levying a comprehensive sales tax on services that is restricted to the retail level alone.[6] It has been argued before that the retailer is the weakest level to rely upon exclusively for the collection of a tax.[7] Even when this risk is accepted for the delivery of goods, the provision of services at the retail stage tends to be both highly fragmented and highly specialized.[8] Thus the administrative difficulty is largely related to assessment and collection procedures. In addition to this in a RST a complicating factor is the mixed use of services. A service may be used for the purposes of taxable transactions,[9] for private

---

4. Both taxes apply the destination principle, are neutral toward the saving-consumption choice and most probably the number of registered firms for the two tax systems are the same (since many wholesalers and manufacturers also make some retail sales and would need to be registered (Tax reform. Sales Tax reform, June 1987. Department of Finance, Canada p. 28).
5. In practice the VAT coverage is also limited by exemptions; their effect however is either cumulation of taxation or a reduced tax burden (*see* Chapter VI.4.4 *supra.*).
6. Cnossen, *op. cit.* note 1 *supra*, p. 596.
7. Chapter VIII. *supra*, note 13.
8. *See* S. Cnossen, *Excise Systems: A Global Study of the Selective Taxation of Goods and Services*, Baltimore 1977, pp. 30–32.
9. I.e. for intermediate use.

consumption purposes or for export purposes. Suspension[10] of the tax between retailers will therefore present inextricable complications; but inclusion of services in the tax without applying the suspension rule will lead to cascading problems.[11] This difficulty[12] to include services in the tax base necessarily results in (relatively) higher rates on goods[13] and a more regressive tax since by its nature services are purchased to a larger extent by higher income individuals and families.[14]

A VAT-technique provides a much better way of including services in the tax base. By virtues of its spread collection technique and its policing nature the risk of noncompliance (exclusively) at the retail stage is largely reduced. Additionally, the eventual use by the purchaser is of no concern to the supplier. It is the purchaser who, eventually, will have to give proof to the tax auditor whether and to which degree he was entitled to deduct the input tax on services rendered to him.

The coverage of a (retail) sales tax has not only a horizontal level (relating to the question whether all supplies of goods *and* services are covered by the tax) but also a vertical level (that is the rate structure and the extent to which derogations and exemptions are permitted).[15]

Under both systems of sales taxation only one rate is the simplest and most efficient structure. Nevertheless, under both systems tax jurisdictions generally apply rate differentiations, based on considerations of social policy.[16] Since these rate differentiations are influenced to a large extent by parochial political considerations, it suffices to observe that in both systems of levying the application of multiple rates results in high(er) perception costs, carried by taxable persons, in a greater risk of misclassification and evasion and in distortions of consumption decisions.

10. Under a RST the purchaser entitled to suspension must provide an exemption certificate; the seller must check the genuinity of the provided certificate.
11. Cnossen, *op. cit.* note 1 *supra*, p. 597. Ironically enough the exclusion of services leads to its own type of complications, caused by the rules for including or separating the service element from the delivery of a good. S. Cnossen, 'Sales Taxation in OECD Member Countries', *Bulletin for International Fiscal Documentation* 1983, p. 158. *See also* Chapter IV.2.3 *supra*.
12. *See* for example the problems regarding taxing services in Florida. G. Mundstock, 'Florida Services: You Only Tax Twice?' *Tax Notes* 1987, p. 1137.
13. Or inherently a weaker capacity to generate tax money.
14. Sales Tax Administration/UN-study, p. 72.
15. Not to be confused with the vertical coverage of a sales tax in general, relating to the coverage of production-distribution sequence.
16. Generally outright exemptions are used under a RST. *See* for the effect of exemptions under a VAT Chapter VI. 4.4 *supra*.

XIII.2.2 Imports and Exports

Both the 'indirect' character[17] and the criterion of external neutrality require that a sales tax applies the destination principle. Ideally exports are freed completely of tax and imports are taxed exactly the same as comparable domestically produced goods. It has been argued (Chapter XI) that under a RST border tax adjustments are hardly necessary, since the need for taxing imports is less important, when there is no lag between the levy and consumption. This, however, does not mean that a RST is by definition (externally) neutral. The problem with a RST is, that it is not capable of freeing exports of tax, since the RST does not only apply to goods (and certain services) destined for sale to consumers but also to certain business inputs, which are not covered by the suspension rule. As a result exporters are paying hidden taxes, of which the burden may be significant, that are not imposed in other countries with a more efficient sales tax system.[18] Another consequence is that imports are treated preferentially, to the extent that the imported goods (taxed at the same rate as identical or similar domestically produced goods) are freed completely of tax upon departure in the exporting country.

The VAT-mechanism is fully equipped to guarantee neutral border tax adjustments. In practice a VAT too will not completely free exports, since exempt (intermediate) services will result in some cumulation (*see* Chapter VI *supra*). To a large extent this can be avoided by sophisticated rules on the place of service, as in article 9 of the Sixth Directive (*see* Chapter VIII. 6.5 *supra*) resulting in zero-rating (intermediate) services, which are exported.

The impact on imports and exports is not only caused, as I believe, by higher distortions of neutrality in a RST, but also by the level of rate(s). Given the inherent administrative difficulty of levying a tax on services and given the concentration of the burden of collection on one (and the weakest) stage in the production-distribution sequence, a retail sales tax is less capable of generating a large tax yield, since the rates are inherently low. Therefore the introduction of a RST is less suitable than a VAT to offset changes in other taxes, for example a corporate income tax or a payroll tax, provided the latter are shifted to consumers.[19] Some improvement in the balance of payment may occur when a VAT is introduced,[20] since a VAT is subject to

17. *See* Chapter II *supra*, further elaborated under the benefit-principle in Chapter X.
18. An example of the effect of hidden taxes is offered in the Canadian report on tax reform (*op. cit.* note 4 *supra*, p. 15.) In Canada, under the present manufacturer's sales tax (MST) the tax on business inputs represents an indirect charge estimated at about 0.9 per cent of the sales value of exports. This amount may seem small but it represents a very substantial fraction – well in excess of 10 per cent – of the profit margins of many Canadian exporters.
19. Which is a reasonable assumption, *see* Chapter II.4 *supra* esp. note 20.
20. Or when the rates are raised, as frequently has been the case in the EC.

the destination principle and payroll – and corporate income taxes are not.[21]

External neutrality and the destination principle are not only matters affecting international trade. Also, these issues affect *inter-state trade* at a national (or supranational) level. At first sight a RST creates the least complications, it is destination based virtually by definition.[22] However, jurisdictional problems, for example in the US and Canada,[23] relating to the allocation of the tax for purchases outside a state, indicate that a RST is not necessarily free of the anathema of intra-jurisdictional border tax adjustments. As a matter of fact (even a limited) expansion of the tax base with some services aggravates the allocation problems disproportionately.[24] I suggest that also in a destination based retail sales tax system inter-state cooperation and coordination becomes inevitable. Once this tuning of retail sales tax systems to each other has become a necessity, I believe the step to a truly broad based tax, the VAT, will be not too difficult if not necessary. Especially since the solutions at a supra-national level for the allocation of VAT (as suggested in the Chapters XI and XII) seem equally suitable[25] for use at an inter-state level (e.g. in the USA's federal or Canada's confederal systems).

XIII.3 TECHNIQUES OF LEVYING

The difference of VAT, as a multi-stage sales tax and the retail sales tax is one of degree. However, the retail sales tax, by virtue of its technique of levying, has a greater susceptibility to non compliance.[26]

VAT, by dispersing the collection of the tax over a number of points, reduces both the incentive to misreport and the revenue consequences of misreporting. Also, the availability of input tax credits on business purchases encourages accurate reporting.[27] On balance a VAT is superior to a RST in

---

21. Adjustments of the exchange rates will most probably adjust the advantages to a large extent, it remains to be seen whether these adjustments can be offset against initial benefits e.g. the conquering of a segment of the foreign market. This is not necessarily a plea to introduce a VAT based on the argument, that it might improve the balance of trade. If this would be the only argument, it would be tantamount to the tail wagging the dog.
22. Cnossen, *op. cit.* note 1 *supra*, p. 603.
23. *See* for example: 'Sales taxes: Rep. Dongan says ways – means to mark up bill requiring out-of-state sellers to collect taxes', *Daily Tax Report*, 2 September 1987, no. 169, 9–1.
24. In case of the Florida service tax the problems caused by this tax have been described as a result of "quick-fix tax policies", however, at the same time interstate cooperation is suggested. *Tax Notes* 2 November 1987, p. 556, McKee and Quick Propose Model State Sales Tax on Services.
25. I do not share McLure's conclusion that if states are intent on imposing value added taxes, the avoidance of fiscal frontiers requires that the *origin* principle be employed. Charles E. McLure, State and Federal Relations in the Taxation of Value Added, *The journal of Corporation Law* 1980, p. 135.
26. Canadian report on tax reform, *op. cit.* note 4 *supra*, p. 27.
27. *Idem* p. 28.

this regard. In addition, an often underestimated advantage of VAT over RST is the "spill-over" from VAT-accounts to audits for income tax purposes. VAT is paid and claimed based on invoices, which are identical for sellers and buyers. Thus, their books of accounts provide to the tax administration a clear audit trail, with the possibility of cross-checks, also creating an effective method to integrate VAT and income tax audits. VAT, therefore, is largely self-enforcing by nature, one of its key advantages over RST.

XIII.4 EXEMPTIONS

Since a VAT, which includes the retail stage, is conceptually not different from a single levy at the retail stage the advantages and disadvantages of a VAT – as described in Chapter VI *supra* – are generally a matter of degree. Only VAT's capacity to generate revenue is reiterated here; for some this makes VAT in its own right superior, for others just rejectionable.

In this final section one aspect deserves further attention, since it is a serious problem within VAT, created by the exemptions. Exemptions necessitate segregating and tracking separately the input tax attributable to exempt activities in the accounts.[28] I believe this is a serious problem in VAT and should not be underestimated. But, without trying to play it down, it should be realized that under a RST inputs, purchased under the suspension rule, must be segregated in the accounts and separately tracked, in order to avoid tax-free private consumption. Under VAT this segregation is related not only to exempt but also to private use, making it seemingly even more difficult. Many exempt activities, however, like hospital care, educational activities, insurance, banking and financial activities are performed on an exclusive basis (i.e. only exempt activities are performed) or by entities (in general corporations or foundations) that have no private sphere, resulting in the same accounting burden as for regular taxable persons, engaged in taxed activities. Of course, most of these problems can be avoided by designing a VAT without exemptions.[29] In most tax jurisdictions the decisive factors to introduce exemptions nevertheless are social policy considerations and anticipated administrative problems caused by taxing certain activities.[30]

On the whole comparing the VAT and RST, the VAT is, in my opinion, superior. It is my firm belief that for most tax jurisdictions, still relying on a RST, the question is not if, but when they will introduce a VAT. Like the cold in winter, VAT is hard to keep away from.

---

28. And this is further complicated by levies on internal production, which allow initially total deduction and eventually a total or partial payment of tax due. *See* Chapter VI.4.4 *supra*.
29. *See* the Canadian report on tax reform, *op. cit.* note 4 *supra*.
30. *See* for further references Cnossen, *op. cit.* note 1 *supra*, pp. 598–600.

Index

INDEX

158